THE CHURCH IN MISSION

THE CHURCH IN MISSION

A Short History of
The United Methodist Church
in Zimbabwe, 1897–1997

JOHN WESLEY Z. KUREWA

Abingdon Press
Nashville

THE CHURCH IN MISSION:
A SHORT HISTORY OF THE UNITED METHODIST CHURCH
IN ZIMBABWE, 1897–1997

Library of Congress Cataloging-in-Publication Data

Kurewa, John Wesley Zwomunondiita.
   The church in mission: a short history of the United Methodist
Church in Zimbabwe, 1897–1997 / John Wesley Z. Kurewa.
      p.   cm.
   Includes bibliographic references and index.
   ISBN 0-687-01033-0 (alk. paper)
   1. United Methodist Church (U.S.). Zimbabwe Conference—
History. 2. Methodist Church—Zimbabwe—History.
3. Zimbabwe—Church history.   I. Title.
BX8382.2.A45Z59   1997
287'.6—dc21   96-46514
                                                          CIP

This book is printed on recycled, acid-free,
elemental-chlorine–free paper.

97 98 99 00 01 02 03 04 05 06 — 10 9 8 7 6 5 4 3 2 1

MANUFACTURED IN THE UNITED STATES OF AMERICA

CONTENTS

Foreword

This book should be interesting reading for Christians of main-line denominations, independent churches, and students of the Christian faith on the African continent. It addresses issues of the historical, theological, and developmental consciousness of The United Methodist Church in Zimbabwe. This consciousness begins with the introduction of the Christian faith to the African and, hence, the encounter of that new faith with the African culture. Dr. Kurewa is correct in pointing out that early Methodist missionaries, like other missionaries of that era, equated African culture with heathenism; as a matter of fact, it was African culture to which they referred as "Dark Africa." Further, the book addresses how the Church as a whole in the 1950s and 1960s accommodated issues of African nationalism, urban mission, and ecumenism, and shows how the Church adjusted itself to a new situation following the Independence of Zimbabwe in 1980.

It is fitting that a book like this is published because the African Church as a whole, including The United Methodist Church, played a significant role in the development of several African nations on this continent. The United Methodist Church in particular has provided novel leadership both in the evangelization of the people of Africa as well as in conscientizing people to their social and human rights. That novelty has been shared by proclaiming the whole gospel to the whole person.

Finally, this book addresses the issue of how the Church both in Zimbabwe and on the whole continent should continue in the process of adjusting itself to the constantly changing mission; namely, the African reality in relation to evangelization, Africanization of the faith, and church participation in nation-building programs. Happily, such participation in nation-building programs by churches is not a new task for the African churches, because from the beginning of Christianity in Africa, the Church has always been involved in programs of education, health care, and development, especially in rural areas. However, what is needed, according to Dr. Kurewa, is a new theological understanding of this partnership between the Church and secular agencies, like African governments—the two being understood as co-workers in God's mission instead of the Church maintaining the status quo.

It is my hope that all who have an interest in knowing how churches have developed from the status of missions to churches with mission in Africa will find reading this book to be rewarding.

The Reverend Christopher Jokomo
Resident Bishop
The United Methodist Church
Zimbabwe

Preface

In December 1997, The United Methodist Church in Zimbabwe will celebrate the centennial anniversary of Bishop Joseph Hartzell's arrival in the country. Although United Methodism missionary work in Southeast Africa was part of the Congo Mission Conference until 1901,[1] the origin of The United Methodist Church (which was then the Methodist Episcopal Church) in Zimbabwe was associated with Bishop Hartzell who arrived in the country on 10 December 1897.[2] The celebration of Bishop Hartzell's arrival in the country to start missionary work suggests that the United Methodist Church in Zimbabwe is beginning to be aware of its own history and tradition.

The thesis of this book is that a historical and theological self-consciousness is essential for the Church in Africa today. As the simple and homogeneous life that characterized rural Africa for several centuries is rapidly being replaced by a more complex way of life, combining urban technology with foreign and new cultures, it becomes especially important for the Church in Africa to be conscious of its own identity.

The Church in Africa has indeed been aware of the changes in recent years and has taken time to study some of the new forces at both national and international levels in order to understand God's mission in the midst of change. While the understanding of issues and forces that affect the life of people is important for the Church in Africa, the point I seek to emphasize is that it is equally essential for the Church in Africa to be self-conscious historically, in order not only to perceive its mission but also to fulfill it. Though I have limited the scope of my investigation to The United Methodist Church, the exercise is also likely to shed light on other churches, not only in Zimbabwe but in Africa as a whole.

I begin by establishing the historical context of the Church from 1897 to 1997. I believe there is a strong and convincing rationale for this approach. There are many people who want to think of

Africa like Janus, the two-faced Roman god—the old and the new; the rural face looks backward at a seemingly unchanging past and the urban face looks forward with hope to the emergence of Africa as a world force.[3] Yet I would like to suggest that these two faces are really one face. The face of Africa that looks forward is the same face that is looking into the past for its own identity and self-consciousness. Here we find ourselves sharing Eugen Rosenstock-Heussy's belief that "The true past points into a new future; revolutions project their political programs into a distant past."[4]

Immediately we are confronted by an inescapable theological implication, namely that the significance and meaningfulness of Christian eschatology to the Church of Christ is due to God's act in the incarnate Word. In the event of the Incarnation the Church finds a living faith (1 Cor. 15:14), and in Christian eschatology the Church finds a living hope (1 Cor. 15:23). Thus, as Jürgen Moltmann asserts, while faith binds persons to Christ, hope sets faith open to the comprehensive future of Christ. Faith and hope in Christ are inseparable companions and the one does not make sense without the other.[5] In fact, in order for us to understand the present it is important to know the past, which we need to know precisely for the sake of the future.

This is the relevant point: With a history of one hundred years and its own heritage, The United Methodist Church in Zimbabwe needs to take its history and tradition very seriously in order to remain in relation to both the future and the past as they determine or break into the present. To be more specific, The United Methodist Church in Zimbabwe today needs to accept critically both its early missionaries and African leaders, both clergy and laity, as its spiritual fathers and to make every effort to understand those leaders. Those leaders had their own theological motivations for the work they did. Since today's church leaders build on their work it is very important to make every effort to understand them for the sake of our historical and theological self-consciousness. Thus the rationale for establishing the historical context is that a deep look into the past and into the tradition of The United Methodist Church in Zimbabwe is necessary for the Church to understand and prepare itself to face the open-ended present and to fulfill its mission.

The primary source materials for this book were the official journals of the East Central Africa Mission Conference (1901–1915), the Rhodesia Mission Conference (1916–1930), the Rhodesian Annual Conference (1931–1979) and the Zimbabwe Annual Conference (1980–1996) of The United Methodist Church in Zimbabwe. Unless otherwise indicated, the reader should assume that presented information is from these sources.

The use of journals for this study might suggest that I am restricting myself to very limited sources. Yet in fact these journals contain an amazing amount of information, much of it previously unused as primary source material. These journals give us access to the dynamic interactions in the life of the Church. We hear missionaries, of course, but for the first time, we hear the African voices, too, the African voices of non-ordained evangelists with whom missionaries labored side by side and whose names may never be found in other documents. When those African evangelists called their own people "heathens," "kaffir," or "boys," it helps us understand what was going on in the life of the Church, especially as African believers imitated missionaries in theologizing.

There are three parts to this book: *The Church in Missionary Thrust (1897–1921)*; *The Church as an Institution (1921–1945)*; and *The Church in Mission (1945–1997)*. The first two parts are divided because: (1) there was no written constitution of church organizations before the year 1921 in the journals and (2) the first African minister to be ordained in the Rhodesia Annual Conference was David Mandisodza in the year 1921. Similarly, the second part is separated from the third because (1) all Constitutions of church organizations within the then Methodist Episcopal Church in Rhodesia were written in the journals between the years 1921 and 1945, with the exception of the then Methodist Youth Fellowship constitution which appeared in the journal of 1957; and (2) generally speaking, with the end of World War II in 1945, even in South Africa where white supremacy was still in effect until 1994, things could not possibly remain the same. Two points are worth mentioning about the period beginning with 1945. First, the sixth Pan-African Congress that met in Manchester in 1945 caused many repercussions in the political life of Africa. At that congress W. E. B. DuBois, an African American, was a great inspiration to leaders like Kwame Nkrumah, and Jomo Kenyatta.[6] Second, within Zimbabwe the new African National Congress of Southern Rhodesia (a black political party) was not formed until 1957. However, long before that time there was a spirit of unrest at work in the land. Just as it was a new era for the rest of the world, so it was for the Church.

The United Methodist Church in Zimbabwe has been very accepting of some of the forces of the new era, some of which have come into existence as a result of the preaching of the gospel.

These temporal divisions are not entirely a creation of the Church; they are also a consequence of situations in which the Church found itself. The Church need not be ashamed of the fact that its presence in Africa as a living agent brought about many changes in the lives of the African people.

Finally, many reasons could be given to stress the importance of this type of study for the Church in Zimbabwe, and indeed, for Africa as a whole. But four reasons suffice. First, it is vital for any Church of Jesus Christ in Africa to remind itself that it belongs to God (1 Cor. 3:9; Gal. 6:16), and that its very existence is by God's action (Acts 20:28; 1 Pet. 2:5). Many churches in Africa have gone through difficult times: political turmoil in the country; unnecessary divisions, at times caused by personality differences; violation of human rights; and many others. What a renewal of spirit it might bring to such a church to remind itself, that in spite of the harshness of life and the subsequent suffering, its existence in that country can only be explained by God's action.

Second, this kind of study enables the Church to examine itself and find to what extent it has identified with the cultural life of the people it is serving. For example, with The United Methodist Church, a hundred years of history is now a long enough time for critical self-evaluation. Churches in the Third World have had a way of thriving on the cultural and traditional patterns of the missionaries who brought them the gospel, without realizing the importance of their own indigenous ways of life. The result is that the Church has too long remained foreign to the people, or, as a distinguished Nigerian theologian put it, the Church in Africa has been speaking to Africans in strange tongues. African cultural identity is essential if the Church is going to communicate and theologize with the people it is serving.

Third, any church in Africa needs to understand itself in relation to the ecumenical spirit that is pervasive not only in its own country, but on the entire continent of Africa. The multiplicity of churches in Africa is a matter of no little concern. Yet the spirit of ecumenicity in the African Church has been one of the most encouraging signs during the last four decades; common projects and unity talks have been going on in different regions and cities

14

among different churches. In the pursuit for unity among churches in Africa, can ways be found to make negotiations more intelligible, participatory, and profitable than has been the case in the past? Are the differences that are important to mother churches equally important to the African Church? As we will deal with ecumenical issues later on, at this point it suffices simply to mention again that African churches need to take a critical look at their early denominational missionaries and African leaders who are their spiritual fathers and upon whose shoulders they stand. Church leaders need to understand the theological peculiarity of our fathers in order to participate more effectively and profitably in ecumenical gatherings and talks.

Fourth, as the Church of Jesus Christ comes into existence by God's action, so it must exist for God's mission; never have there been people of God without His mission. God's mission, which is to be understood in the historical context, can never be perceived in the same way through all the ages. Because history is constantly changing, our perception of God's mission must change too. For example, what encouraged Bishop Hartzell to start missionary work in Zimbabwe was the protection he expected from the British flag; yet for over seventy years the same Church, in partnership with several other churches in Zimbabwe, had taken a firm stand against the inhuman treatment of the people governed under the same flag. Now we begin to see the necessity of dialogue with the fathers. For the Church in Africa to begin understanding the new present and to be able to live in it, there is a great need to understand the theological rationale for all that was done by the fathers. The theological self-consciousness that we need will only be attained if the Church is willing to take time to look backward; and only then will it be able to face the future with confidence.

◆ ◆ ◆

I am indebted to several people for many helpful suggestions. They include Professor Egon Gerdes, who originally guided my doctoral thesis at Northwestern University, Evanston, Illinois; and Professors Jean Greenburg, Hoyini Bhila and Ivan Nye, who read the revised and the additional chapters to the original manuscript. It is only natural that our minds could not march together in every particular view that I set out, and they should not, therefore, be held responsible for any such views. I am also indebted to my two secretaries, Susan Chaya and Nyaradzo Madzongwe, for typing the draft and final manuscripts respectively, and to my wife, Gertrude, for her encouragement and patience as I worked on this book.

John Wesley Z. Kurewa
Vice-Chancellor, Africa University
Old Mutare
20 January 1996

Part I

The Church in Missionary Thrust (1897–1921)

During this period, The United Methodist Church was known as The Methodist Episcopal Church. Similarly, the countries Zimbabwe and Mozambique were known respectively as Southern Rhodesia (popularly known as Rhodesia), and Southeast Africa.

Chapter 1

The Historical Background

To write a complete history of the Christian thought of United Methodism in Africa is beyond the scope of this book. But some historical background is needed to enable us to see how United Methodism, as we know it today, was introduced in Africa and how it spread to different countries, including Zimbabwe. All Methodist Episcopal Church work in Africa (with the exception of Liberia which from the beginning was a conference unto itself), was under the supervision of one bishop and was known until 1891 as the Congo Mission Conference.

The Methodist Episcopal Church in Africa

The Methodist Episcopal Church (now The United Methodist Church) came to Africa by way of Liberia through an American settlement of freed slaves in the year 1822.[1] Among the first American Negro immigrants who settled in Liberia was a large group of Methodists with a lay preacher, Daniel Coker, who organized them into a Society and thus became the founder of the Methodist Episcopal Church in Liberia.[2] The first Methodist Episcopal Church missionary to arrive in Liberia on 8 March 1833 was Melville Cox. Thereafter a number of missionaries were sent to continue the work among the new settlers. After a period of over sixty years of Methodism in Liberia, a petition from the Liberia Conference was presented at the 1884 General Conference in Philadelphia asking for a missionary bishop who would reside in Africa.[3] With reluctance, the request was eventually granted at the same General Conference, with the election and consecration of William Taylor as the first missionary bishop of Africa.

Bishop Taylor is believed to have had a plan for planting a chain of mission stations across Africa from the west to the southeast as a way of preventing Islam's encroachment further south. In his writing, this idea was supported by the Bishop's own frequent use of the phrase, "a chain of missions," and in actuality the plan was evident by the way he planted missions from Angola in the west to Mozambique in the southeast of Africa.

With the heroic leadership and self-sacrifice of Bishop Taylor a new interest was awakened in the evangelization of Africa. Accompanied by forty-two men, women, and children, he landed in Angola on 20 March 1885.[4] Angola was already under Portuguese control; the first Methodist Episcopal Church mission station, St. Paul de Luanda, was established in the capital city of Luanda that same year. Later, several other stations were opened inland (Dondo, Nhanguepepo, Pungo Andongo, and Malange). In September 1885 Bishop Taylor made a quick trip to Lisbon where he met the king of Portugal, and to Brussels where he met the patron sovereign of the Congo, Leopold II. These contacts enabled Bishop Taylor to enter the lower Congo River and establish another chain of mission stations.

In visiting Portugal, the Bishop was interested not only in expanding his work in Angola. He knew that Southeast Africa was also under the Portuguese flag and when the time was ripe Bishop Taylor appointed Reverend Erwin Richards in Southeast Africa to plant and develop a chain of mission stations there, starting at Inhambane (located in the southern part of Mozambique) and moving into the area south of the Zambezi River.

Apparently Erwin Richards was in Gazaland, south of Mutare in Zimbabwe, as early as 1880, "when the heathen King Umzila was still supreme in the land." At the 1901 East Central Africa Mission Conference, Richards claimed that King Umzila

> offered up his songs of praise and petitions to Almighty God that He would speedily open wide doors and bring in His Living Gospel, both in the form of the written parchment, and of the living missionary.[5]

He went further to say:

> On the tenth day of October, 1881, between the hours of five and six p.m., Umzila King of Gazaland at the royal kraal of Umoya muhla, granted his official sanction for the initiation of what had become the East Central Africa Mission Conference of the Methodist Episcopal Church.[6]

Unfortunately, Richards does not tell us more about his activities or those of the American Board of Foreign Missions, which sent

20

him to Umzila's country to explore the possibility of establishing missions under its aegis. What is clear is that, in 1881, Richards and another missionary were sent by the American Board to Inhambane, in the southern part of Southeast Africa, to start missionary work among the African people. Due to some linguistic, political, and climactic difficulties created by the geographical location of Inhambane, the American Board decided to abandon work in Inhambane and move inland to Gazaland in the eastern region of Rhodesia.

A missionary known as Dr. John Goucher of Baltimore had spent long hours with Bishop Taylor persuading him to begin active missionary operations in East Africa. A few days after those discussions, Bishop Taylor was petitioned to take over the work at Inhambane Mission, an offer that he accepted, probably with some pleasure, given his dream to form a chain of missions across the continent.

Richards must not have been happy with the decision by the American Board to abandon work in Inhambane, for he decided to join the Methodists who were taking over work at Inhambane. On Christmas Eve 1890, Richards (of Oberlin College, Ohio) was commissioned the first missionary of The Methodist Episcopal Church in Southeast Africa.

During the period of Bishop Taylor's supervision of work in Africa, Richards mentions three accomplishments at Inhambane: the acquisition of titles to three of the stations; the re-purchase of every item of former mission property; and the continuation of the usual religious services in two of the Methodist stations.

Richards must have encountered difficulties. There were no funds forthcoming; and the four missionaries who were sent as reinforcements left within a year. However, he found consolation as he labored side by side with two faithful African colleagues, Tizore Navess who was stationed at Makodweni and Sikobeli Muti at Kambini, neither of whom received any remuneration then. The four missionaries who arrived at Inhambane on 9 December 1982 included Erwin Richards (who had returned to the United States for a short time), Mrs. Richards, his wife, who was coming to Southeast Africa for the first time, and A. L. Buckwalter and his wife; the latter were forced to return to the United States shortly after their arrival because of the continuous ill-health of Mrs. Buckwalter. Yet for all this, Inhambane Mission thrived under the leadership of Richards who worked closely with the African evangelists Tizore Navess and Sikobeli Muti.

The United Methodist Church in Sierra Leone came into being as a result of the union of The Methodist and The Evangelical United Brethren Churches in 1968. Similarly, "The former Evangelical Episcopal Church in Burundi became part of the United Methodist Church in 1984. Early in 1980, the Ekan-Muri Church in Nigeria had also done the same."[7]

The Methodist Episcopal Church in Rhodesia

In 1886 Bishop Taylor retired and Joseph Hartzell was elected to succeed him as Bishop in Africa. Apparently, long before his election, Hartzell had been keeping abreast of events on the African continent, carefully following the colonial movements. His records inform us, for example, that he had read a carefully prepared essay on the Partition of Africa in 1885, and had acquainted himself with the map of the continent so thoroughly that it had become part of his knowledge.

The development that excited the newly elected Bishop was the northward movement of the British flag, from South Africa to the regions beyond the Limpopo River. It was Cecil Rhodes, after whom Zimbabwe was named Rhodesia, who was a pivotal force behind that northward movement of the British flag. Rhodes had already found his fortune in the diamond and gold mines of South Africa and he was personally in a strong position to be able to finance the white settlement north of the Limpopo River (now Zimbabwe). In addition to his interest in the wealth that could be found in those regions, Rhodes, a staunch British imperialist, was also interested in using those same regions as a route to move further north. His dream was to see a chain of British colonies established from the Cape to Cairo; Bishop Taylor meanwhile spoke of planting a chain of mission stations across Africa from west to the southeast. Bishop Hartzell relates his London breakfast conversation with Cecil Rhodes in which the Bishop asked Rhodes what his chief ambition was in life. The latter replied:

> My ambition is two-fold: (a) to do the greatest possible thing for barbaric humanity, and (b) to do all in my power to promote the unity of the English-speaking races of the world. When that unity is a fact, there will be no more war.[8]

The Bishop's understanding of Rhodes' philosophy was that for him to realize his first ambition, Rhodes truly believed "British control would be a blessing to the African." Regarding the second ambition, Bishop Hartzell points out that it was Rhodes' belief that Great Britain and the United States of America should stick together in all they did. Consequently, Rhodes left eight million dollars to establish about a hundred scholarships annually for American scholars to study at Oxford University.[9]

One appreciates Bishop Hartzell's understanding of Rhodes' mind and thinking. Indeed, it must have been through those kinds of associations that Bishop Hartzell was successful in negotiating his plans with Rhodes. Rhodes must have told him about his ambition to establish a chain of British colonies from the Cape to Cairo, and Bishop Hartzell sought to tie in that northward movement of the British flag with the Methodist Episcopal Church missionary work:

> During the cheering which followed the announcement of my election as a missionary Bishop for Africa, at Cleveland, Ohio, in May, 1896, and before I was invited to the platform, the following words were distinctly impressed upon my mind, "Somewhere in South Africa in the midst of the advancing waves of Anglo-Saxon civilization northward and under the British flag, American Methodism should have missionary work."[10]

Following his election Bishop Hartzell made his episcopal visits to Liberia, Angola, and the Congo. September of 1897 found him in England where he was joined by Mrs. Hartzell from America, and together they left for South Africa. While in Cape Town, Bishop Hartzell was able to meet Rhodes, and Rhodes invited the Bishop[11] to attend the celebration for the completion of the railroad from Cape Town to Bulawayo (now the second largest city in Zimbabwe), located in the western part of the country. Bishop Hartzell accepted the invitation and entered Zimbabwe for the first time in October 1897. On returning to South Africa, Bishop and Mrs. Hartzell visited Kimberley, Johannesburg, Pretoria, and some other places of interest. After that brief visit to South Africa they traveled by sea to Beira, a port town in Mozambique located about two hundred miles from Mutare, now the main city in the eastern region of Zimbabwe.

After the white settlers had constructed the railroad they discovered that a range of mountains lay between it and Mutare;

Rhodes consequently ordered the small town to be moved to a site where the railroad could reach it. New Mutare was established sixteen kilometers south of the older site.

It is not known exactly when and where Bishop Hartzell first learned about the transfer of Mutare town from one site to the other. One could only speculate that it could have been at one of the three places where he was with Rhodes: when they met for breakfast in London, when Bishop Hartzell saw Rhodes in Cape Town, or when Hartzell was invited to travel along with Rhodes to the celebrations in Bulawayo. Of course, it could have been on all these occasions that they talked about this issue of such importance to Bishop Hartzell's efforts to start the Methodist Episcopal Church missionary work under the British flag.

When Bishop and Mrs. Hartzell left Beira for Mutare, ready to make their second entry into the country, the rainy season had already begun; before leaving Beira they learned that the newly built railroad had been washed away by heavy rains in several places. Nevertheless, they managed to travel by rail to Macequece (now Villa Perry), a distance of about 280 kilometers from Beira, being carried by African laborers over the washouts.

Because the railroad from Macequece and Mutare was still incomplete, Mrs. Hartzell remained in Macequece in a mud hotel, and the Bishop traveled alone the last forty kilometers to Mutare on a horse that had been loaned to him by the Portuguese governor of Southeast Africa. As the Bishop approached Mutare, he must have been deeply impressed with what he saw, for he wrote:

> After a horse-back ride of twenty-five miles through mud and rain and crossing swollen rivers, I caught my first sight of the Mutare valley. The view was from the mountain pass. The valley was 3300 feet above the level of the sea and the thriving village in the distance on which the sun was shining, with the mountains surrounding, made a picture of restful beauty. The words that thrilled me at Cleveland came again, and I said, "There, or somewhere near, is the place."[12]

In words reminiscent of Paul in his letter to the Galatians (4:12-13), Bishop Hartzell described the state of his appearance as he entered the village of Mutare: "I rode into Mutare a stranger, weary and hungry, soaked with rain and bespattered with mud; but if ever a Methodist preacher was led by God, I believe I was, in coming to Mutare."[13]

Bishop Hartzell discovered that the village already had several hundred European settlers, all of whom had come from the another village that had been abandoned. Mutare, surrounded by picturesque mountains, was not only beautiful, as the Bishop discovered, it was also healthful because of its high altitude. Further, he must have been pleased by the fact that the great wave of migration of Europeans into that region was under the protection of the British flag; and the only church that he found in the new village was that of the Church of England. Through the combination of these factors, Bishop Hartzell became convinced that "Here is the place for a great central Mission among Europeans and natives."[14]

On Sunday, 12 December 1897, two days after his arrival, the Bishop conducted two services. The first was held in the morning in a large office of a Dutch trading store and was attended by a number of Europeans. An attempt to secure some hymn books from a missionary of the Church of England was turned down, so the group had to settle on old familiar hymns that they could sing from memory.[15] The second worship service was held that same evening in a room of a company building that belonged to Messrs. Wm. Phillipi & Co. (which later became the workshop of Puzey and Payne—a well-known service station in Mutare to this day).

Bishop Hartzell started negotiations with the British South Africa Company toward the establishment of a mission center. In his request for a place to start a Methodist Episcopal Church Mission Center, he dealt mainly with three persons: the administrator of Mutare, Captain Turner; the administrator of Rhodesia, Earl Grey; and Cecil Rhodes himself—clearly all quite influential people. Bishop Hartzell was obviously an accomplished leader who moved with confidence in the corridors of power as an ambassador for Christ.

It is said that at about the time when the town of Mutare was in the process of transferring from the old site to the new, a question was put to Rhodes concerning what he was going to do with the old site, to which he replied, "We will turn it into a Mission." Whether Rhodes knew at that point about Hartzell's request we do not know. Happily, Bishop Hartzell received a letter from Earl Grey dated 21 March 1898 saying that the Bishop's request had been granted; he was to receive the old site of Mutare, which had thirteen thousand acres of land. In addition to the land, the old site had several buildings "worth at least $65,000 and the stock, mechanical shops, outfit, etc., certainly $10,000 more," reported the Bishop. Additional land to begin missionary work at the new site was also given to the Bishop.

The offer of land by the British South Africa Company was contingent on two conditions: the establishment of a school for Europeans in New Mutare and the planting of a large and well-equipped industrial mission for Africans at Old Mutare. These conditions became open doors of challenge and mission for the Methodist Episcopal Church.

Organizing a Mission Conference in Rhodesia

The date of 16 November 1901 was an historical moment for The Methodist Episcopal Church in Africa, especially in the southeastern region. At 9:00 a.m. on that day, a Saturday, at the Mutare Academy Building, (the present site of the United Methodist Inner City Buildings in Mutare) Bishop Hartzell took the chair. Delegates had come from Inhambane, Southeast Africa, and Rhodesia. The Bishop opened the session by reading Isaiah 35:1-10 and Acts 2:1-15, after which was sung "The Church's One Foundation Is Jesus Christ Her Lord." After a prayer the Bishop preached.

As already noted, with the exception of Liberia, all Methodist Episcopal Church missionary work in Africa was known as the Congo Mission Conference. However, the General Conference which met in Chicago in May 1900 resolved that two conferences be created out of the Congo Mission Conference: the East Central Africa Mission Conference, which included the work in East Africa south of the equator; and the West Africa Central Africa Mission Conference, which included work in West Africa south of the equator. Together Rhodesia and Inhambane comprised what came to be known as the East Central Africa Mission Conference. In accordance with the General Conference action, Bishop Hartzell, who had convened the first session of the East Central Africa Mission Conference on 16 November 1901 in Mutare, Zimbabwe, declared that all former members of the Congo Mission Conference who were then in that part of Africa belonged to the East Central Africa Mission Conference. In fact, this affected only three members of the mission conference:

26

Erwin Richards, an elder in full connection
Morris Ehnes, a probationer
James DeWitt, a probationer

The following were received by transfer:

Robert Wodehouse, from the Texas Conference
Frank Wolf, from Cleveland, Ohio
John Springer, from Chicago, Illinois

The following missionaries were present:

Eddy Horace Greeley
George Odlum
Herman Heinkel
Mrs. J. L. DeWitt
Miss Harriette Johnstone
Mrs. Helen Rasmussen
Mrs. Erwin Richards
Mrs. Robert Wodehouse
Mrs. Frank Wolf

The following Africans were present:

Tizore Navess
Charles Yafele
George Muponda

On a lighter note, James DeWitt presented a gavel to Bishop Hartzell. The gavel was made of the wood of a gun taken from the Africans during the Matebele Revolt in 1896. In accepting the gavel, the Bishop spoke of the appropriateness of the gift at the time of the first session of the East Central Africa Mission Conference, and expressed the hope that the memento would be used by officers presiding in succeeding sessions.

To crown it all, on Sunday, 17 November 1901, at 2:30 P.M., Bishop Hartzell, with all the mission conference delegates, dedicated the first African Chapel to be constructed by any of the predecessor bodies of The United Methodist Church in Zimbabwe. The church was primarily for African employees who worked in European stores and did domestic work for the new settlers. That congregation contributed $50 toward the construction of the church.

Summary

(1) The founding of The Methodist Episcopal Church chain of missions seems providential, judging by some of the missions' origins. It is particularly notable that it was Africans freed from the world of slavery who came to Liberia with the new faith. Hence, missionaries or no missionaries, Africa was clearly already in God's plan to hear the gospel. Further, the way Bishop Taylor took over missionary work in Inhambane area is impressive, as is the manner in which Bishop Hartzell was led to take over a vacated town for The Methodist Episcopal Church in the Mutare area.

(2) It appears that the heroic and evangelistic leadership of Bishop Taylor in Africa, which resulted in the formation of a chain of missions, later suffered from lack of personnel and funds. The idea of missionaries being self-supporting suffered a setback. Nonetheless, the very fact that Bishop Taylor introduced the idea of self-support at the outset is impressive.

(3) Bishop Hartzell seems to have dealt effectively with top government officials concerning the support of church missions. Indeed, in its resolutions, the third session of the East Central Africa Mission Conference of 1905 noted the Bishop's skillful manner in handling negotiations and the respect and favor in which he was held by government officials.

(4) Though The Methodist Episcopal Church was initially introduced into Africa by Africans returning from the world of slavery, indigenous African leadership quickly emerged and participated in the launching of The Methodist Episcopal Church in Southeast Africa and Rhodesia. We have noted how Sikobeli Muti and Tizore Navess labored faithfully side by side with Erwin Richards in the Inhambane area, and also that Navess and George Muponda participated in the deliberations of the first session of the East Central Africa Mission Conference in 1901 in Mutare. Muponda was a teacher at the Mutare Methodist Episcopal Church, and also served the Church as an interpreter, having received his education at Lovedale in South Africa. During that first mission conference session, both Navess and Muponda gave a personal testimony of their Christian conversion, as did all missionaries.

Chapter 2

The Planting of Mission Stations

Mission stations were particularly a characteristic of Christianity introduced by missionaries coming from northern developed countries to Third World countries. Such missionaries were motivated either by colonial settlers migrating to new countries or purely by their own religious conviction. Upon their arrival in the mission field, they either found a mission station where they were to stay, or they would start one. Those mission stations served multipurpose functions.

We have already found that Bishop Taylor labored tirelessly to start a chain of missions across Africa in order to prevent Islam encroaching further into the southern part of Africa. However, most missionaries viewed mission stations as a base from which the evangelistic, educational, and health care programs of the Church were planned and implemented for the surrounding areas. In recent years, some of those mission stations have developed into great institutions of education and/or health care for the local people.

Mission stations were also places where missionaries found protection from outsiders. Most of the missions had adequate communication with representatives of the colonial flag under which they operated. Time and again, missionaries would flee from one country to another and would go to the mission stations for protection; in this way the missionaries would minister to one another. By the same token, several nationals found refuge in mission stations. In Africa, a young woman who refused to be married as a second or third wife could seek refuge in a mission station where she found sympathy and protection from such harsh traditional customs. In addition, orphans found a new home in mission stations. That having been said, we shall now turn to the planting of the five United Methodist mission stations in Zimbabwe.

Old Mutare Mission

Today, Old Mutare towers majestically as the Jerusalem of United Methodism in the country. It was the first mission station to be started in Zimbabwe, as already noted by agreement of Bishop Hartzell and the British South Africa Company in 1898. Old Mutare gradually became a leading center for evangelism, education, and health care in the eastern region of Zimbabwe. In 1989, Hartzell High School at Old Mutare produced the best results in the Province of Manicaland. Out of 104 Hartzell High School students who wrote Form Six examinations to qualify for entry at the University of Zimbabwe, 102 passed; and out of the 2,400 students who started the undergraduate program at the University of Zimbabwe, 79 had come from Hartzell High School. Needless to say, Old Mutare is the location for the new Africa University, which was established by The United Methodist Church for the whole of Africa. The choice of Old Mutare for this purpose could not have been better; for it is both an historical center and has already proved to be a sound educational center.

The official opening of Old Mutare Mission was on 7 October 1898. On that occasion, Bishop Hartzell preached on the text: "Fear not little flock, for it is your Father's good pleasure to give you the Kingdom" (Luke 12:22). The first person to do active missionary work at Old Mutare was Reverend M. H. Reid. He was never a regularly appointed missionary, but was employed by the Mission, and had arrived at the same time as Reverend Morris Ehnes in 1898. The two were soon to be joined by Reverend and Mrs. James DeWitt of Ohio Wesleyan University, Mrs. Anna Arndt, and her assistant, Herman Heinkel. These were the missionaries who, after white settlers left for the new town, cleaned up the mission, cultivated the land, taught, and preached until the inauguration of the conference in November 1901.

Old Mutare Mission was founded with the primary purpose of establishing an industrial education center. Apparently, it was Eddy Greeley who started the boys' school at Old Mutare in 1901. He had been a missionary in Liberia, where his first wife died, as well as the husband of Anna Arndt, whom he married upon her arrival in Zimbabwe.

The first male student at Old Mutare was known as Kaduku. Unfortunately, he died while still a student and was buried at the mission cemetery. The enrollment of male students had increased from ten in 1901 to forty in 1903. A few of those students were taking what were already considered to be advanced classes. The appearance of the first female students at Old Mutare was reported by Helen Springer at the third session of the mission conference in 1905 when she said:

> We have now five young girls all engaged to our own boys and are bright and promising. They study only the vernacular, reading, writing, and arithmetic, sewing and housework.[1]

By the time of the 1907 conference, V. R. Swormstedt reported:

> We began our work at Hartzell Villa, August 2, 1905, having been transferred by Bishop Hartzell from Inhambane to Old Mutare. On that date Bishop Hartzell gave to the W.F.M.S. some thirty-five acres in land and a building valued at $6,500 for which we desire to express our sincere appreciation. Our predecessor gave over nine girls, two married women and two babies. With this outfit we opened a girls' school.[2]

Therefore, we can safely say that by 1905 there were female students at Old Mutare Mission; and that they could have started soon after the Second Session held from 29 September to 7 October 1903. Although we are not given names of the first female students, we know that some of them were among the list of "Bible Women" of the 1909 report that included the following: Mufambiswa Caplen, Fumendiswa Chimbadzwa, Mutiziswa Peranyi, Mukonyerwa Mari, Mary Matimba, and Matingapasi Sakutombo.

Church work at Old Mutare was focussed on students or the training of those who were to go out as pastor-teachers. As the title suggests, such students were to be equipped for their training as teachers as well as pastors or evangelists to communities they served. They were the real extension of mission outreach to villages. However, we note that pastors at Old Mutare remained missionaries for a long time during that period of growth and expansion of The Methodist Episcopal Church.

Mutambara Mission

In 1905 Robert Wodehouse, with an unnamed African evangelist, visited Chief Mutambara's place about eighty kilometers south of Mutare. The chief immediately invited Wodehouse to start a mission station in his area and the government gave its consent. Two factors impressed Wodehouse on the three visits he made to Chief Mutambara's place during 1905: the large population and the fertile land. A year later The Methodist Episcopal Church officially obtained land at Mutambara.

John Mazonya, a pastor-teacher, or evangelist was appointed to work at Mutambara Mission before Wodehouse arrived there in 1905. Later in 1908 he was joined by three missionaries: A. L. Buckwalter and his wife, and Edith Bell. A school was started immediately in which Mrs. Buckwalter taught the boys and Miss Bell taught the girls. According to the report of T. A. O'Farrell, who was appointed to Mutambara after the Buckwalters were sent back to America because of illness, evangelistic work in the out-stations surrounding the Mutambara area was mainly left to African evangelists, while missionaries were involved in the technical business of running the mission. This observation is noteworthy because often the evangelization of Africans tends to be too exclusively associated with missionary names and visits.

Murewa Mission

In June 1905, John Springer had made a trip from Gandanzara to Murewa with ten students. That October he made another quick visit to Murewa accompanied by his wife. People in Murewa already had had contact with government officials and traders but not with missionaries.

In June 1908, E. L. Sechrist, an industrial school missionary-teacher at Old Mutare, went up to Murewa and stayed in the area for three months evangelizing among the people. Murewa is 256 kilometers northwest of Old Mutare and about 90 kilometers north of Harare. In the same year Dr. Samuel Gurney also went to Murewa. He was a missionary medical doctor who came to Rhodesia in 1903 and was one of the missionary pioneers responsible for the opening of The Methodist Episcopal Church work in the Murewa, Mutoko, and Nyadiri areas.

Although Dr. Gurney's work was much appreciated by both African and white farmers in the Murewa area, the efforts to open and establish a Methodist Episcopal Church mission station in the area met with resistance from the chief right from the beginning. The government had a standing policy that missions should not be forced upon the people and therefore the chief's consent had to be obtained before applying to the government for a site and official documentation. Although the people appreciated the services of Dr. Gurney, the chief consistently refused the idea of a mission station.

Both the Roman Catholic and the Anglican Churches had earlier been denied entry into the area. Several meetings between the native commissioner at Murewa and the chief took place in hopes of changing the chief's mind. But the chief insisted, "My heart does not want a mission in my country." Eventually the native commissioner referred the matter to the Native Department of the government in Salisbury and from there it was referred to His Honor the Administrator, with the recommendation that authority be given to the Native Department (in that special case) to grant mission sites even though the chief refused his consent. Apparently the people wanted the mission, so perhaps this action was appropriate. Authority was readily given and the first site was given to The Methodist Episcopal Church to start a mission station. In his report to the annual conference, Dr. Gurney exhorted, "And so the whole country is before us, and we are now at liberty to 'go up and possess it.'"

Two mission stations were opened in the Murewa area. The first one was Kanyasa Mission, which soon closed because of the lack of missionary personnel and the chief's attitude toward the whole thing; the mission no longer exists. The second was the Murewa Mission, which has grown to be one of the leading mission centers in the country. The Murewa Mission site had been occupied by a trader; after his death the place reverted to the government, which in turn gave it to The Methodist Episcopal Church in 1909. A mission station was officially opened that year. It is difficult to ascertain why the chief in the Murewa area was not willing to have mission stations in his area. It may have been because of earlier unfavorable contacts with the white people, but we do not know for sure. One thing we do know: if the government had a policy that missions should not be forced upon people, as Dr. Gurney informs us, then the chief's decision was not respected. Here is an incident where the Church has rightly been criticized for its alliance with the colonial powers.

Mutoko Mission

In his report of 1910 Dr. Gurney emphasized that Mutoko, about sixty-five kilometers north of Murewa, was a very strategic place for a mission station mainly because of the large population in that area. Early in 1911 the government gave the old police camp, which contained several good brick buildings, to The Methodist Episcopal Church to start missionary work in the area. Very little was done at Mutoko until 1915 when an African teacher, Isaiah Kashayan-yama (Isaiah Munjoma), was appointed to this place. After another two years the place began to deteriorate again. Wilfred Bourgaize is associated with the revival of the work in the Mutoko area; he stayed there from 1922 until his retirement in 1957. Bourgaize was unique in that, unlike other missionaries, he never owned a car; he did a lot of walking to open new places. In his 1923 report to the annual conference he maintained before his colleagues that Mutoko was the most densely populated area, with the largest villages he had ever seen any place where the mission conference was working; yet very little had been done by way of sending teachers to open schools and start churches in villages. "Calls are coming in from every direction, 'Send us a teacher'," Bourgaize exhorted the conference. Bourgaize equated the people's call with the Macedonian call that Paul heard (Acts 16:9).

This cry for "a teacher" is a phenomenon that had been characteristic of the Church in Africa. Wherever the chief or people asked for the Church to come into their village, it was not always clear whether they were seeking the proclamation of the gospel or a school. Probably we are safe in saying that the invitation implied both. Proclamation of the gospel and education were both considered good news by the African people but missionaries wanted to separate the two. Professor T. O. Ranger reminds us of the Church slogans; with the Catholics it was, "Who owns the schools will own Africa" and with Protestants, "Use the school to build the Church."[3] This desire and invitation for schools became a real challenge.

Nyadiri Mission

The Nyadiri Mission, forty kilometers north of Murewa was acquired on 16 August 1922, and immediately work began with Dr. Gurney, I. E. Tull, and Job Tsiga. Sekuru (uncle) Tsiga, as he was popularly known in the mission conference, died in 1975, and was greatly respected for his long service in the hospital at Nyadiri. He is reported to have been working with Dr. Gurney in the Murewa area in 1908. The emphasis of work at the Nyadiri Mission from the beginning was medical work, including a dispensary building built in 1923. It is not surprising that Nyadiri stands today as the center of the annual conference's medical work; not only when counting the number of patient beds but also when considering the training program for nurses. A school for girls only was started at Nyadiri in 1925; a boys' school was started later. Like the other mission stations, Nyadiri was surrounded by a large population of African people and from there evangelists, teachers and nurses were sent out for Christian ministry.

These five mission stations stand to this day as great centers for the work which is now The United Methodist Church in Zimbabwe. With the exception of Mutoko, these mission stations also stand as educational centers where high school education is attainable, including Nyamuzuwe Mission which was started in 1957. Yet the mere citation of the facts that these mission centers exist is not enough for our purpose. We need also to reflect on the significance of what was going on as these mission stations were being established.

Summary

(1) Mission stations were bases from which missionaries intended to launch their Christian mission to the rest of the country, within their geographical limits. As the Church grew, each region looked to its mission station for help and for answers to any problems that arose. Old Mutare blossomed as the Jerusalem of the mission conference, for it was the place where the annual conference meetings were held until other mission stations, in turn, later invited the annual conference to have its sessions at their places. Before that time, Old Mutare was regarded as the place of authority. Still, whether mission stations fulfilled their original intent or not is a question to keep in mind as we study the life of the Church in the chapters that follow. While it is not my intention to answer the question conclusively, we can look at signs of success, such as the reports of the frequency with which missionaries are going out accompanied by nameless African evangelists, and the speed at

which new churches and schools are opened in the surrounding region. Or to make a reverse observation, the mission stations were not yet too sophisticated to tie people down and hinder them from going out to the task of evangelization.

(2) Another factor to be noted was the cooperation of the Church with the government in the opening of mission stations. Of the five mission stations mentioned, three of them (Old Mutare, Murewa, and Mutoko) were originally abandoned places, generously turned over to The Methodist Episcopal Church to be used as mission stations in those respective regions. It is not surprising that Bishop Hartzell said that The Methodist Episcopal Church was to be congratulated upon its relations with the government. In 1909 one of the mission conference resolutions was an assurance to the government of the Church's hearty cooperation; but we cannot help raising the critical question of whether the cooperation was between government and the Church as a whole, or just between the missionaries and the government. Indeed, judging by the way things eventually developed, the latter would seem to have been the case.

(3) The chief was a key figure in the strategy of the mission enterprise in Rhodesia. For legal purposes his consent was theoretically important, and for practical purposes his consent was a guarantee for an audience.

(4) While many African personnel were involved in the origin of The Methodist Episcopal Church, in the process of planting mission stations, very often only missionary names were attached to the events, with phrases like "and the native workers" tagged on. It is very rare to find African names mentioned; Africans are always in the background. Yet if much of the opening of new congregations in the out-station depended upon unordained evangelists, they were certainly at the cutting edge of the ministry of the Church. It is time to familiarize The United Methodist Church of Zimbabwe with its early preachers, like Charles Yafele, John Malgas at Mutare, William Yafele at Penhalonga, and many others. If, for instance, this could be done through the Sunday School lessons, it would be a helpful step toward true self-identity.

Chapter 3

The "Dark Continent"

When the first East Central Africa Mission Conference of The Methodist Episcopal Church was convened in Mutare by Bishop Hartzell in 1901, fifteen missionaries and two Africans participated, along with several African observers. That number included men and women, members of the conference and nonmembers, clergy and laity. The people who met in Mutare at that historical moment represented the core of the emerging Methodist Episcopal Church in Portuguese Southeast Africa and Rhodesia. While those people were conscious of the gospel that they had to share with the rest of the people in the continent, the missionaries in particular were also aware of the immensity of the power of what they considered to be their primary enemy: heathenism. Indeed, whether correctly or not, no continent has been more closely associated with the notion of heathenism than Africa; it has been commonly referred to as the "Dark Continent," and at times even as a continent behind God's face. Thus when we discuss heathenism in Africa, we are discussing a subject where the attitudes behind the concepts are crucially important. We shall discuss this chapter under two subheadings: heathenism, or the "Dark Continent," and the mission of liberating people from heathenism.

Heathenism, or the "Dark Continent"

According to current dictionary definitions, the word heathen means: (1) "anyone not a Jew, Christian, or Moslem; a person regarded as irreligious, uncivilized"; (2) "an irreligious or unenlightened person, an unconverted individual of a people that do not acknowledge the God of the Bible; one who is neither a Jew, Christian, nor Muslim: pagan." Therefore, heathenism is "a belief or practice of heathens; pagan worship; idolatry; irreligious; barbaric morals or behavior; paganism." The term heathen "is usually used to indicate someone who is hostile toward religion, while a pagan is someone who simply refuses to become interested." With these definitions in mind we need to turn to the conception of heathenism or "Dark Continent" as used in reference to Africa by missionaries and, to a large extent, by the churches from which the missionaries came.

F. D. Wolf, a medical doctor and one of the fifteen Methodist Episcopal Church missionaries who attended the first East Central Africa Mission Conference in Zimbabwe, probably spoke for a number of people when she said "missions and heathen" were two words that she remembered hearing in the days of her youth. Professor Wilson Naylor of Lawrence College in Wisconsin wrote an article on Africa in 1918, after he had visited Africa, in which he defined what he considered to be the manifold meaning of the term "Dark Continent." He wrote that in addition to the fact that the African people were of dark color, they were also devoted to dark customs and practices; and that Africa was a land where even religion was a thing of darkness. The term "Dark Continent" was a regular reference to Africa by early missionaries as revealed in "A General and Historical Statement of Methodist Episcopal Missions in East Central Africa" report to the East Central Africa Mission Conference by Emory Beetham who said, "November 16, 1901, is a significant date in the history of Methodism in the 'Dark Continent.'" Likewise, in his personal report to the same conference, Beetham is recorded as saying that he had been invited to consult with Bishop Hartzell concerning educational work in the "Dark Continent."

A missionary who found himself assigned to Africa thus naturally thought of heathenism as the primary enemy of his work. This heathenism was vividly portrayed by missionaries. Eddy Greeley, who arrived in Rhodesia in 1900 after a brief stay in Liberia, described his visits to villages: "As I entered kraal after kraal, all in dense darkness of heathenism, my soul was overwhelmed with the awful responsibility resting upon everyone bearing the name Christian."[1] Similarly, John Gates, who came to Rhodesia from the Rock River Conference in Illinois in 1907 and, as one of the more articulate missionaries, is quoted frequently, wrote: "Upon no other continent or island has Satan such a vast array of fiendish forces—the horrors of pre-historic ignorance, superstition and savagism."[2]

Although one wishes that Gates had further explained what he only implied in the various terms, the main point is clear. He portrays the "ugliness" of heathenism in Africa as perceived by white outsiders. For example, African marriage laws and practices were viewed with contemptuous suspicion by missionary churches; consequently, in the first conference convened in the country, the categorization of polygamists in a sub-probationers class was approved without serious consideration. In the case of illness in the family, consulting a medicine-man or herbalist was prohibited as a heathen practice.

To talk of heathenism in Africa or of the "Dark Continent," or of the African people as living in darkness was synonymous with the idea that Africans were people without any culture or civilization. We have already noticed how the colonial settlers, like Rhodes, thought of the white man's presence in Rhodesia as a way of promoting Western civilization. Whether white settlers agreed with the goals of the missionary enterprise or not, at least they interpreted the missionary presence in Rhodesia as necessary for the purpose of civilizing African people. A good example is a quotation from the Earl Grey, then Administrator of Rhodesia, in his letter to Bishop Hartzell:

> My colleagues and I view with great satisfaction your desire to establish an important center of your Church in Rhodesia territory. We heartily welcome the cooperation of your countrymen, and are particularly glad to receive your assurances that it is the wish of the United States to take an active part with England in her endeavors to establish the rules and security of Anglo-Saxon civilization in territories which have hitherto been submerged by barbarism.[3]

We need to raise some questions at this stage. For instance, how seriously did the settlers view missionaries as partners in the work of "civilizing" the African people? Did missionaries believe that civilizing African people was part of their missionary work? Bishop Taylor, for one, took this task seriously. For example, he is quoted as saying that one of his episcopal responsibilities in Africa was "to embrace the industries necessary to the self-support of civilized life for all those whom we get saved and civilized."[4] Further, he wrote about establishing a nursery in every mission station where children adopted from heathendom would be brought and nursed before they were old enough to become heathens themselves.

According to Bishop Taylor, this was to provide the children with an exposure to both evangelization and civilization, after

39

which they would be released back into the mainstream of African life. Erwin Richards informs us how enthusiastically they raised African children in their home in Inhambane, with the hope that separating them from heathen home influences and training them in missionary Christian homes would yield refreshing results. Apparently, there were two theories about how to go about it. The first one was

> that our converted and home-trained children, then grown to maturity must live somewhere, somehow, and we early thought they should start homes of their own and live consistent Christian lives and shine as bright lights in the heathen world about them.[5]

But the second theory was a modified one which stated that

> they should take from one to five children into their homes, that these children should dig for their food as they would have to do at home, and in other relations they should not greatly depart from what would be their constant Christian training and early spiritual development till there was formed a little Christian community well worthy the name of Church. But this theory never with all its beauty worked.[6]

We are left with no doubt in our minds that Erwin Richards was implementing Bishop Taylor's theory. It is an interesting observation though, that the same theory was also used in Australia among the Aborigines. Could it be that Bishop Taylor, a widely traveled evangelist who had been to almost every continent before he became Bishop of Africa, was implementing a concept that was prevalent during that era?

While some missionaries may not have agreed with Bishop Taylor, still the two processes of evangelization and civilization became mixed into one. This is further illustrated by an Anglican missionary whose mission station, known as St. Augustine, is about ten kilometers away from Old Mutare. In writing about the 347 people who had come from the surrounding villages to be baptized at St. Augustine, he wrote: "As for what baptism means to them, they all know that Christianity demands a break with heathen customs and the worship of spirits."[7]

Worship had to become Christian; but when Christianity demanded a breaking with heathen customs, who decided which customs were heathen? Because missionaries tended to see heathenism in all that was African, the result was to substitute

Western customs for the African ones. E. L. Sechrist, who taught industrial training at Old Mutare in 1907, observed that the training of African students in agriculture and mechanics, or in housework in missionary homes was a way of civilizing the African while he was being christianized. The point is that intentionally or not, evangelization and civilization (in the sense of attempting to substitute the Western way of life for the African way) went on hand in hand. We must admit there is very little discussion of civilizing the African by most missionaries, who probably had prejudices and made assumptions without having time to reflect about it in writing.

If it were true that missionaries tended to regard everything African as heathen and seemed to substitute Western ways for African ways, the next question we need to ask is: Did missionaries really understand African people? Could they indeed understand them without appreciating their culture? We hear missionaries, like colonialists, calling the African person a "heathen," a "kaffir," a "native," a "boy." Even the early African evangelists adopted the Westerners' terminology and spoke of their own people as "heathens" as they had been taught by their Christian education or theology. This derogatory concept of their own people and their own culture alienated them from their people and culture.

Returning to the definitions: some say a heathen is anyone who is not a Jew, Christian, or Moslem; others that a heathen is an unconverted individual or a people that do not acknowledge the God of the Bible; still others that a heathen is someone who is hostile to religion. Putting these definitions together, a heathen seems to be one who does not acknowledge the God of the Bible, the God recognized by Jews, Christians, and Moslems, or it is one who is hostile to religion. While the West recognized the religions of the East, it did not recognize African tradition and religion. Missionaries were unable to see anything of value in African culture in general or in African traditional religion in particular. Yet are there not some aspects of the African concepts of God which are comparable to Jewish, Christian, or Moslem concepts?

The Mission of Liberating People from Heathenism

Looking at the reports of the missionaries to the conference of 1901 we can make two important observations. First, out of the

fifteen missionaries, nine spoke of a definite conversion experience; one of the two Africans gave a similar testimony. Second,
twelve of the fifteen missionaries spoke of a definite call to be a
missionary. This emphasis on conversion experience and call to
ministry or missionary service set a precedent for the emerging
Methodist Episcopal Church in Rhodesia. Thereafter, anyone
claiming to be a Christian had to point to a definite conversion
experience, and aspiring ministers had to testify to a definite
conversion experience and call to their work. Even today, candidates for the ministry of The United Methodist Church in Zimbabwe are required to share with the Board on Ordained Ministry
both their conversion experience and their call to the ministry.

For the early missionaries the sharing of these experiences
affirmed that they were a new people in Christ Jesus, and, as such,
sent out with a special mission to liberate others who were still
under the bondage of heathenism, using the traditional missionary
methods: evangelism, education, and medicine.

Evangelization

The preaching of the gospel had priority over all other methods
of evangelization in Zimbabwe. John Gates emphasized this point:
"Pulpit preaching is undoubtedly the most potent factor in assisting
the Holy Spirit to bring about immediate, definite decision on the
part of the native to renounce heathenism and take Christ."[8]

But who was to do the preaching? Gates was very clear on that
issue. In the 1912 conference report, he impressed on the conference that the evangelization of the African depended upon the
African himself. Gates must have spoken from the experience we
referred to earlier. As missionaries became more involved with the
technical details of running mission stations, the task of reaching
out to the surrounding villages was left to the African evangelists.
John Springer, as district superintendent of the Mutambara area,
took the same approach. For example, he invited two African
evangelists, Abraham Kawadza and Daniel Caplen, to spend ten
days preaching at the mission center and in the surrounding
villages. Describing how the services were conducted, John Springer says: "There was no formality and the people were free to ask
questions and put up arguments which they did and the Christians
answered them."[9]

These meetings were not limited to church buildings; preachers preached wherever they found people, even at a beer party. Abraham Kawadza, in particular, is said to have been very helpful in this kind of preaching, often speaking from the depth of his own experience and knowledge.

In the process, John Gates came to realize what made a program of evangelism effective. While he was convinced that the African evangelists needed to be dedicated, he also perceived the need for better-trained African evangelists. In 1911, he pleaded with the conference for evangelists who would be able "to face the deadly paganism of Africa," and that they "must be trained and qualified." Gates tried to make sure that he was not misunderstood; he did not want to overemphasize academic training as such. But since The Methodist Episcopal Church depended upon the African evangelist to evangelize the Africans, the Church had to see to it that the African evangelist was adequately trained. Unfortunately few missionaries then shared this insight. Even long after Gates' time, some Western missionaries still believed that they themselves were needed as evangelists in the Third World, rather than as helpers to train people of those lands who could do more effective and lasting work in evangelization.

Group evangelism, a method of evangelization used by The Methodist Episcopal Church in Rhodesia, was a rural and Africanized way of doing evangelism. The initiative came from an evangelist or from a group within the church. Eddy Greeley writes of special evangelistic campaigns where nearly two hundred villages were visited in Chief Marange's area and the program was spearheaded by two conference evangelists but always with a group of volunteers. For instance, by 1907, five hundred members of The Mutare African Church had gone out to share their new faith on their own, at different times, and in various small groups.

In order to understand the implication of group evangelism, it is necessary to delve behind the available written tradition to the oral tradition. Here I shall refer to one of the many stories I have written as a result of conversations with my mother. My mother was converted to Christianity when she was a young girl during the 1918 revival and since then has been vitally involved with Church life. She told me of an incident that happened at Sherukuru Church—our home church. Sherukuru is about forty kilometers north of Old Mutare. The church there was started in 1907. In 1920,

43

the Sherukuru Church lost its pastor-teacher for reasons beyond their control. Naturally, since by that time it was one of the largest congregations, with about six hundred members (both full members and probationers), it was a matter of great concern. In the midst of the resulting confusion, which had generated a sense of hopelessness, a child in the village had a dream. He was told to inform the church to go to Manyarara; the advice was ignored. During the same week, however, another church member named Lawrence Kurewa, (the author's uncle), also had a dream. In his dream he was asked, "Have you done what I told you"? Startled, Lawrence went to see the church lay leader, Martin Mugochi, and told him his story. That evening, Martin Mugochi rang the church bell and when the people of the congregation had gathered, he informed them of this latest development of the child's dream. That very night the Sherukuru Church engaged in prayer, asking God to reveal to them what He wanted them to do. They still did not know where Manyana was. During prayer it occurred to them to go to Nyamukwarara, another Methodist Episcopal congregation some fifty-five kilometers east of Sherukuru, to share their problem with the people there, with the hope that by praying together God would let them know what was meant by the child's dream, as confirmed by the man's dream.

As people were traveling to Nyamukwarara something strange happened. They met Nyamukwarara people on their way to Sherukuru; they too had a dreamer who had told them they were needed at Sherukuru. Nothing more was given to them than the simple fact they were needed at Sherukuru; thus they were on their way there. Together the two groups went to Sherukuru and spent the whole night in prayer at the church and, with the church bells ringing, others came to join them. The following day they all went to Vumbunu, another Methodist Episcopal congregation east of Sherukuru. They told their story to the Vumbunu people and decided to spend another night in prayer at the church. The following day they went to Nyakatsapa, the largest congregation in the area. By the time the big crowd reached Nyakatsapa, the wish of the Sherukuru people for a new pastor had grown to an impressive size. David Sakutombo, the pastor-teacher at Buwu Methodist Episcopal Church, became the spokesman of the group. He approached John Paisley, the resident missionary in that area, also stationed at Nyakatsapa, and told him the story of the Sherukuru people. John Paisley wrote a letter for them to the district superintendent, John Gates at Old Mutare, in which he related the story. The whole group then went down to Old Mutare. After reading the letter, Gates told the Sherukuru people to take Thomas Muziti, a pastor-teacher stationed at Manyarara (about five kilometers from Old Mutare) to Sherukuru as their new pastor. Thus what began as a child's dream was fulfilled.

The author tested the accuracy of his mother's memory by checking names and dates involved; the story is credible beyond dispute. But what is its point? As these people spent several nights in the churches, they were not only praying, they were also preaching, testifying, and singing hymns. Several people were brought in to join the church. People were converted in this way, without pastor-teachers being involved. This is confirmed by many other stories.

Such an approach to evangelism, whether initiated by an evangelist or a group, is particularly rural and African for two reasons. First, meetings are held without time limits. As I have experienced, there are many meetings where people spend the whole night sharing their testimonies, singing, and praying together. Second, the practice of going from one church to another comes directly out of rural African life where people like to do things together, such as helping one another in their fields or raising a new house. Such mutual participation in projects is the African rural way of creating a sense and spirit of community. The practice still prevails and some traditional churches have adopted it. Independent churches in Africa have come to take it very seriously indeed.

Christianity became a true liberating power only when it was permitted to take African forms, such as going from one village to another, from one church to another, and spending the whole night praying and sharing testimonies. In this way Christianity provided the African (in African forms) with something that was not available in traditional religion, which on the whole had remained an affair for spectators. The sense of personal involvement, sharing one's personal concerns, being heard by others through testimonies, and realizing that there were others facing similar problems; all this blossomed under the good news that Christ Jesus had died and was raised in order to be Victor over all the powers that tormented people. Thus God's liberating powers became a reality to many people.

Education

Rhodes' offer to The Methodist Episcopal Church of land and buildings at Old Mutare came with the condition of establishing a school for the white settlers in New Mutare and planting an industrial mission for Africans at Old Mutare. In accepting the offer, The Methodist Episcopal Church underscored its long-term understanding of education as a vital part of its mission in liberating people.

It was not easy to separate evangelistic from educational work during the early missionary days in Rhodesia. One could not stand without the other and both seemed to aim at the same purpose. The Protestant idea was to use the schools in order to build the church; the two were always intertwined. For the Methodists a pattern evolved: Missionaries or African evangelists went out to some remote villages to preach. The chief would then ask missionaries to send a teacher in order to start a school in the village. At times they asked for a church, but very often by a church they meant a school as well. If the missionaries were able to send a teacher, he would actually be a pastor-teacher. It appears that by 1910, people in the village were expected to provide a residence for the teacher, to put up a church building, (which would also be used as a school during the week), and to contribute some money toward the salary of the teacher. Sometimes, like at Marara Methodist Episcopal Church, people could not afford to give money but they arranged to give their teacher food instead. Wherever a teacher was sent by the Church, that teacher also had the responsibility to start a church in that village.

It is crucial to look at the philosophical and theological rationale that The Methodist Episcopal Church employed in its educational program. First, from observations that can be made, education was used as a means to communicate the gospel to the African people. There was no way a missionary could have effectively communicated with the African over a period of time without teaching the African to read. The objective was, of course, to teach the African to read the Scriptures. Thus DeWitt's wife in 1905 reported to the conference that at the boys' school at Old Mutare she limited her instruction almost exclusively to the Bible. In his report to the conference in 1905, John Springer, speaking of the curriculum at Old Mutare, pointed out that out of five subjects

46

taught in school, three reading lessons were devoted to the Bible; the other two subjects were English and Shona. His emphasis was typical of the importance placed on religious instruction in the curriculum. Buckwalter was proud to report that an exceptionally good girl at Mutambara was able to read the whole New Testament in Shona. Education, as perceived by the early missionaries, was basically a way of communicating the gospel to the African people and was not an end in itself.

Second, education became a means of producing African leaders, particularly for the Church. As early as 1907, The Methodist Church was already training teachers who had spent only four years in school. By 1909, only students who were already committed Christians and had indicated some interest in becoming Christian workers would be accepted at Old Mutare. Before that time, many people had come to Old Mutare simply to study English, in order to procure better and supervisory positions, such as in the mines. This was the pattern they saw in the white supervisors and a few African supervisors. As a result, the belief spread that educated people do not work. When missionaries encountered such an understanding of education, they argued that an educated Christian man should be prepared to go out into the village to share not only his academic knowledge but also the saving knowledge of God through Christ Jesus.

Third, right from the beginning there seems to have been a mutual understanding between the government and the different churches, and The Methodist Episcopal Church was not an exception. George Duthie, inspector of the education department, was invited to the first conference of 1901 where he was introduced by Bishop Hartzell. In his brief address to the conference, Duthie gave government assurances of cooperation with the new Church. A few years later, a government official was quoted as saying that the Methodists were the only missionaries who were really pushing things. When government inspectors visited Old Mutare in 1909 the school was recognized as first class, and Old Mutare was given a grant of £99 (about $297).

However, the mutual trust between the government and the Church suffered through several incidents. One of the issues most disturbing to The Methodist Episcopal Church then was the poll tax required of every African male. Most of the students who attended school at these mission stations were mature men, some

47

of them already married; this expectation to pay the tax placed them in a difficult position. Unless someone paid it for them, they had to leave school for a while to work for the money to pay the tax. Missionaries perceived that practice as a most unjust burden imposed upon students.

Another incident arose when it was reported to the conference that the government was spending £200,000 for the education of 30,000 whites, and only £24,000 for 900,000 Africans. John Gates considered it a serious problem to treat whites in a preferential way, particularly since the African students were required to pay the tax.

Finally, education was considered a way of liberating the African. Some of the missionaries, however, became liberated themselves in their own conception of the African. William Terrill and Herbert Howard, both missionaries stationed at Old Mutare spoke about African people in their report, "The State of the Church," the way any white person of the time would have spoken: "We all understand the low condition of the raw heathen and the diminutive mentality of even the best natives."[10] They went on to describe the African as possessed by the demon of ignorance "with his congenital laziness."[11] However, in 1914 Herbert Howard had to return to America for an operation, and while recuperating he enrolled in some courses in psychology and education at Hartford where he gained new insights:

> The desire has grown in my heart and consciousness to know the African better. To know them intimately, adequately, and so far as possible for mortal man thoroughly.[12]

Howard immediately went to work. He challenged his fellow missionaries' interpretation of the African as biased by a Western perspective and unrelated to what the African really was. As a teacher at Old Mutare for many years, Howard was appalled at the curriculum that was so Westernized that it left the African unrelated to life around him. That new insight was unfortunately not shared by many others. How different this was from what Howard had written with Terrill in the "State of the Church" six years previously. Howard was ahead of his time just as John Gates was.

Education was, however, playing its rightful role in laying aside prejudices and for the first time was enabling missionaries to perceive Africans as they really were and to gain a new appreciation of them.

48

Medical Ministry

The name of Dr. Samuel Gurney assumes early importance in the medical program of The Methodist Episcopal Church in Rhodesia. In giving his report to the conference in 1910, Dr. Gurney said:

> Others come up to the Conference reporting many various sheaves which they have gathered from the fields in which they have labored, but the medical missionary can give no such glowing report. He can only tell of the uprooting of noxious weeds, the blasting of rocks, and the preparation of the soil for seed. The harvest is yet all in the future; and so apparently little has been done.[13]

Dr. Gurney's words plunge us immediately into the issue that we need to explore because it is centrally important to our study; namely, the theological rationale for the medical ministry. What is it? Two things must be considered.

First, as in the case of education, The Methodist Episcopal Church was using the healing ministry as a way of preparing people for the gospel. For example, when the Church realized that the chief in Murewa area was not interested in opening doors to missionaries for mission stations, Dr. Gurney was sent there "to see if the ministry of healing might not open the hearts of people and thus prepare them for the reception of the gospel."[14]

Dr. Gurney himself points to this quotation in his report to the conference in saying that his work was a preparation of the soil. We can suppose that many held his view, or simply assume that it was tactical rather than theological.

Second, the Church is aware that at times pain, illness, or disease reduces a person to something less than human; and the Church finds itself in a position where it must alleviate the pain— because it cares. It is this kind of motivation that has kept mission hospitals in a vital ministry in Zimbabwe and Africa to this day. Such an approach to the healing ministry does not exclude doors that might be opened for gospel communication. While the tendency in the early days of the Church was to prepare people for the gospel, the idea of healing people for their own sake was not entirely absent either. It would be an exaggeration to attempt to make a clear distinction. The main point is that through the healing ministry people realized the love of God and were thankful. Eddy

49

Greely, who cured many people, reported that some of these people began to pray for some more medicine while others brought corn and goats to him as their expression of gratitude. This was a typical African way of expressing gratitude among the Shona. A goat is always the most appropriate gift to the medicine-man and it was always sent after the patient was cured; in that way it became an expression of gratitude and not an expected fee.

The earlier missionaries, in identifying the enemy as heathenism, remained faithful to the old missionary methods: evangelization, education, and medical work. Statistically, by the year 1921 the Methodist Church had 2,465 full members and 2,100 probationers. The Church was managing eighty-three elementary schools with 4,873 pupils; there were seventeen missionaries, one ordained African minister, and eighty-four unordained African workers. Unfortunately, conference statistics do not show us how many hospitals or clinics existed in 1921.

Two critical questions remain. First, did the West use the term "heathenism" incorrectly in reference to the African people? Is it not unfortunate that missionaries did not study African traditional religion as seriously as they did the religions of the East? Second, while the missionary enterprise in Africa was indeed a mission of liberation, the missionaries saw the African as being in need of liberation from heathenism; did that not mislead them into identifying Christian liberation with the Western way of life?

Summary

(1) The Western and missionary conception of Africa as the "Dark Continent" and the conception of African culture as heathen and even to regard culture or civilization as absent in the history of African people was indeed more of the former's attitude than the reality that came out of enlightened study.

(2) Evangelization, education, and medical care by missionaries among the African people became the foundation of the development of African people into a new way of life.

(3) If colonial settlers and missionaries did not share identical objectives in their presence in Africa, they apparently shared the concept of civilizing (whatever they meant by that) the African. That way of thinking led to the mistaken idea of adopting Western ways of life as the Christian way.

Chapter 4

The Expansion of Methodism and African Leadership

On the occasion of the creation of the East Central Africa Mission Conference in Mutare, which included the Districts of Inhambane and Mutare, a significant number of African leaders were already in church service. A perusal of the relevant documents reveals that in 1901 there were already the following pastor-teachers in the Inhambane District: Fanrangwani, Matewu, Sikobeli Muti, Angilazi, Kaliji, Tizore Navess, Josiah Hayes, Xinzabani Hayes, and a printer, Gigalamugyo. In the Rhodesian District, Charles Yafele is the only one listed as an appointed pastor-teacher; but George Muponda, a teacher who assisted with interpretation in the Mutare African Church every Sunday, was also present at that first conference.

As the purpose of this chapter is to relate the expansion of Methodism to the emerging African leadership in the Rhodesia district of the East Central Africa Mission Conference, the Inhambane District will only be referred to from time to time since the two districts were under one mission conference until 1915.

There were three waves of movement in the expansion of The Methodist Episcopal Church in Rhodesia, although the third one was not realized as had been planned. These movements of expansion were: the southward expansion, the northward expansion, and expansion toward the Zambezi River.

The Southward Expansion

The expansion of The Methodist Episcopal Church to the south radiated from Mutare. We have already noted that the transfer of Mutare Town from the Old Mutare to the new site in 1896 was immediately followed by the construction of a pole and mud church building for Africans in New Mutare; that first church building was dedicated by Bishop Hartzell in 1901. The site of the church was at the corner of Second Street and East Avenue, and remained in that locality until 1940. However, in 1905 the pole and mud building was replaced by a small brick church building which was unfortunately blown down by the whirlwind in 1912. With the implementation of the Land Apportionment Act (1931), which was a demand by white Rhodesian farmers for the separation of white and black land, the African congregation was moved from what had become white land to the hilltop in Sakubva Township. The old site was allocated for colored and Indian work. Charles Yafele, a South African evangelist, was the first pastor-teacher to work with the Mutare African congregation.

As the church continued its expansion southward, the first place to be evangelized was Penhalonga, sixteen kilometers north of Mutare. This has since become a large mining area that originally had been prospected and developed by the Portuguese towards the turn of the nineteenth century. The Portuguese lost the mines to the British South Africa Company in a war that occurred between the two as a result of a rivalry for mineral concessions in Manicaland. During the first decade of the twentieth century more and more gold prospectors and miners found their way to Penhalonga to mine and pan for gold. This resulted in thousands of Africans being employed in gold mines; in 1905 there were about two thousand African workers at two mines at Penhalonga who came from all parts of the country and from various tribes.

Charles Yafele, who had an effective ministry in Mutare, was moved to Penhalonga in 1905. By 1907 two strong congregations were established. Two commodious church buildings had already been built, one on the Penhalonga Compound and the other at Rezende Compound.[1] The church buildings cost over $2,000. A day school for the children and a night school for the mine workers were established and Charles Yafele was in charge of both schools. Robert Wodehouse spoke highly of Charles Yafele's evangelistic preaching both in Mutare and Penhalonga. Conversions were reported to have occurred continuously in his ministry.

Although Charles Yafele was succeeded by William Yafele in Mutare in 1905, William Yafele's ministry in Mutare was very brief. In the same year, soon after the small brick church had been constructed in Mutare, another South African evangelist, John Malgas, a colored man, was appointed as pastor-teacher. The Mutare congregation flourished and expanded its membership so much that it found itself in need of a bigger church building. Robert Wodehouse described John Malgas as a zealous and faithful preacher. It is further reported that not less than five hundred members of this Mutare congregation went out to share the light and that some of the best young leaders in the early life of The Methodist Episcopal Church in Rhodesia came from that congregation. By 1908, about eight leaders worked in the Mutare District while many others went to Old Mutare Mission for training. Unfortunately, John Malgas' ministry in Mutare was short-lived. He uttered the following words on his deathbed:

> My end has come. Soon I am going above where God is. I want to leave this testimony, that it may be told to my brothers. God called me to the work of preaching the Gospel. My work is now finished. My soul is in peace and my heart is washed in the blood of the lamb. I have nothing against any man. I was glad to preach the Gospel. Now my end has come and God is with me and I am very happy. I have seen the heavenly Temple. There were no doors. I saw many people. They were of all colors. Each had an open book in his hand. Although there were so many yet the House was not full. It was God's Temple, the home He has prepared for me.[2]

The southward expansion of The Methodist Episcopal Church gave birth to a new and important mission station at Muradzikwa where a congregation was established in 1904 with the assistance of the chief. Another South African evangelist, David Ntuli was appointed at Muradzikwa, about twenty kilometers south of Mutare. Ntuli reported several conversions to Christianity and also established a very successful school attended by as many as one hundred children. Ntuli was also known for his pastoral visits in the neighborhood. Muradzikwa United Methodist Church has remained a leading congregation in the area to this day.

Mutambara, another important station about seventy-two kilometers south of Mutare, was opened in 1905. The area was populous, fertile, and well watered by two rivers. This Mutambara area had been set aside by the Southern Rhodesia government for the exclusive settlement of Africans. The growth of The Methodist Episcopal Church at Mutambara was largely due to African initiative. In 1905 Bishop Hartzell appointed Stephen Tiki, a local man, to preach at the mission station and in the surrounding area. However, very little is known about his ministry or his achievements beyond the fact that he was there until 1907 when another local man, John Mazonya, replaced him. It is interesting to note that Mazonya claimed fame for being the first African convert in Mutare in 1901 under the ministry of Charles Yafele. By 1903 Mazonya had already become a full-fledged preacher. The development of evangelism, education, and health care at Mutambara Mission has been attributed to these two African preachers, Stephen Tiki and John Mazonya. However, they share fame with the first missionaries who were appointed to Mutambara in 1908, namely A. L. Buckwalter and his wife, M. B. Spears, and Edith Bell.

William Yafele had been moved to Muradzikwa in Chief Zimunya's area by 1908. He is said to have been an excellent linguist speaking Shona, Xhosa, Zulu, Nyubi, and English. In addition to his pastoral and teaching responsibilities he found time to translate parts of Scriptures; in 1907 he had finished translating the psalms.

Sub-Chief Muyarari to Zimunya, whose area is about sixteen kilometers south of Muradzikwa, had presented a request for a teacher in his area in 1908. Subsequently, the Bishop appointed Gezana Sadomba to start work at Munyarari in 1909. Munyarari Church commanded a very strategic position for the expansion of The Methodist Episcopal Church in the whole area. Although we do not know much about the achievements of Sadomba, the area of Munyarari has to this day remained a United Methodist stronghold.

Further, by 1909 Eddy Greeley had been appointed to work in Chief Marange's area southwest of Munyarari, where he is reported to have been dearly loved by the people. According to Robert Wodehouse, Greeley's popularity was due to the fact that he healed the sick and wounded. Chief Marange took a leading role in encouraging the establishment of both the church and school in his area. A church building was built at Mount Makomwe, a site chosen by the chief himself. It is not surprising that the Marange Chieftainship has strongly supported The United Methodist Church to this day.

One of the African leaders who is reported to have worked hand in hand with Eddy Greeley in Chief Marange's area was David Mandisodza. His specialty was hymn-writing. In his report to the conference, Greeley wrote: "One lad, Mandara has written two hymns without help. David Mandisodza has been of much help in

54

hymn-writing."[3] David Mandisodza spoke for himself before the Bishop at the 1908 conference when he said:

> When I came to the Mission I did not know how to read or interpret or preach or teach. So, Mr. Greeley taught me all these things and the Lord has been my helper too. When God sent me among the heathen I found them very cheeky . . . [4]

In his report to the conference in 1917, Eddy Greeley disclosed the author of a hymn that has been a source of great inspiration to all generations of United Methodists in Zimbabwe to this day. The hymn was written to a tune typical of the African rhythm. The words are as follows:

> Ndofamba, ndofamba
> Ndosuwa Kudenga
> Kunyika yaTenzi
> Isina nenhamo.

The hymn was written by Jonas Mandara Manjengwa, as was the tune.

A significant development during the period of the planting and establishment of The Methodist Episcopal Church was the emergence of independent preachers, meaning African preachers whom Methodist missionaries found already preaching to their own people entirely at their own initiative. A notable example of these independent preachers in the southern region was Johannes Chimene who eventually joined The Methodist Episcopal Church. Johannes Chimene, son of a chief, was converted to Christianity while in the Transvaal, South Africa, where he worked in the mines. Upon his return to his home, Fort Victoria (now Masvingo) in the southern part of Zimbabwe, he began preaching to his people with great passion. In June 1906 when Robert Wodehouse and Eddy Greeley visited the Masvingo area intending to open new stations, they found Johannes Chimene in the area preaching the gospel of Christ. He joined The Methodist Episcopal Church at the invitation of Robert Wodehouse. At the 1909 annual conference, Johannes Chimene had this to say:

> I have been preaching and praying with my people all the time. They are asking for the way now. The people are calling for the teachers. They say that the darkness is great.[5]

The Northward Expansion

The expansion of Methodism to the north also radiated from Old Mutare. The African initiative in this as in all other cases is difficult to identify because of the terminology used in the literature of the time which described Africans as "native assistance" or "native helpers." However, it is clear that their role as interpreters greatly facilitated the spread of Methodism among Africans, for the missionaries knew almost nothing about the places where they went preaching the gospel and the presence of African interpreters and/or preachers helped to remove African suspicion of "strangers" among them. In some cases the missionaries sent African pastors to work among their own people with minimum supervision. All that was required of them was to report back to the headquarters at Old Mutare. There are examples of African evangelists who were assigned to work in the small churches surrounding Old Mutare such as Manyarara, Mandiambira, Premier Estate, and Chikanga.

The activities of The Methodist Episcopal Church also spread north of Old Mutare. The missionaries were attracted to King Mutasa's royal court for two main reasons: first, the presence of a large African population in that area, and second, the possibility of exploiting the king's authority and influence over his subjects. There are two cases to illustrate this point, involving missionaries Eddy H. Greeley and Samuel Gurney.

In 1904 Eddy H. Greeley, among the missionaries to have opened the doors of Old Mutare Mission School to the first student intake, visited King Mutasa to start missionary work in what he called "the largest town in Manicaland." He spent a few months teaching Africans Christian songs, and healing them of ulcers, burns, cuts, and other diseases, some of which were chronic and acute. This made a great impression on the king. Henceforth the missionaries worked hard to consolidate the gains they had made at Mutasa's royal court.

The second case involved Samuel Gurney, the missionary doctor, who spent six weeks at the king's royal court studying the manners of the people, their religion, and their attitude toward whites. He wrote down his impressions, some of which read:

> This town is the center of their government; and although the Chief has little legal authority he has great moral influence over the people, and if the leaven is set to work in his kraal it will soon be felt all over

the country. It is an important center for a missionary, and we ought to begin our work at Mutasa's at a very early date.[6]

The rapid expansion of The Methodist Episcopal Church in the Mutasa area is best illustrated by the Conference Statistics of 1908 Session, indicated below:

Mutasa Village	1000
Sherukuru	600
Chikanga	400
Manyarara	300
Vumbunu	200
Mandiambira	100
Muredzwa	100

The manner in which Methodism was introduced in the Sherukuru area clearly demonstrates the role of both chiefs and African evangelists in propagating the gospel in their areas during those early days. Sherukuru United Methodist Church derived its name from the title by which the chieftess of the area was and still is called. In Manyika traditions, Sherukuru is a daughter of Mutasa known as *muzvare* (a royal daughter) in Chimanyika, and from time immemorial that area has always been under a chieftess. A report presented to the 1908 mission conference about the Chieftess Sherukuru had this to say:

This Chieftess is the sister of the former King and is a superior native woman. She is head of a part of the Inyanga District. At the Natives' request we opened work among them and it promises large. Congregation number 600 and over 72 are in school, 140 in Sunday School and a class of 40 will shortly be received on probation. The workers' house is complete and a Church is supported by the Switzerland Conference.

King Mutasa was responsible for the introduction of United Methodism in the Sherukuru area. In 1907 Chakanyuka, the reigning Mutasa went to Sherukuru with some of his counselors and some African evangelists, including Samuel Matimba who was then based at Mutasa's royal court. There was no missionary present. King Mutasa himself introduced The Methodist Episcopal Church to the Chieftess Sherukuru, who in turn did the same to the headman of the village, Chivutabure or Kambanga, popularly known as Kurewa, an uncle of the author. My mother, who was then about seven years old, still recalls a song which Matimba taught the people at the introduction of The United Methodist Church at Sherukuru. The song is as follows:

> Pindukayi madziMambo
> Pindukayi maDzishe
> Jesu watipindukayi
> Muchida kuendawo kudenga
> Mwari wati pindukayi.

> Repent Chiefs
> Repent Sub-Chiefs
> Jesus says repent
> If you want to go to heaven
> God says you must repent.

Another interesting factor about Sherukuru was the pastor-teachers who were appointed there. Phillip Perayi was the first pastor-teacher who stayed at Sherukuru until 1909, when he had to leave because of illness. He was succeeded by Peter Jamakanga in 1910 and Aaron Vigor, who both originally came from Mozambique. We also discovered that some of the first preachers in The Methodist Episcopal Church in Rhodesia came from South Africa.

The next important area to be penetrated by United Methodism was that presided over by Chief Makoni of the Waungwe people who lived about sixty-four kilometers northwest of Old Mutare. United Methodism was propagated in Chief Makoni's area at a fairly early stage of the establishment of The Methodist Episcopal Church. Daniel Caplen, an evangelist, was the first to explore the possibility of starting both educational and church work among the Waungwe. We know very little about his activities. However, following the meeting of the mission conference in June 1905, John Springer, a Presiding Elder of the Mutare District, accompanied by ten students, left Old Mutare Mission for a northward exploration. The first heavily populated village they came to was Gandanzara, a sub-chief to Chief Makoni. Then and there, Sub-Chief Gandanzara invited The Methodist Episcopal Church to establish its presence in his area and specifically requested for a teacher to be sent to his village. We are not told the names of the ten students who accompanied Springer on the northward exploration but it is possible that Daniel Caplen could have been one of them. The report presented at the 1908 mission conference shows that at least two Methodist Episcopal congregations had been established in the

Makoni area, the one at Gandanzara with a membership of 800 followers while the one at Svikiro had 540.

When the missionaries went to Makoni's area they found an African preacher already well established there. Nehemiah Machakaire had been converted to Christianity by the Wesleyan Church, (Methodist Church of Zimbabwe) in Salisbury, then the capital city of the colony of Southern Rhodesia. He went back to his home, Muziti, in Makoni area and started preaching to the people about his new faith. Many people were converted and he built a church big enough to accommodate between six hundred and seven hundred people. When Eddy Greeley visited Muziti, presumably in 1907 or 1908, he found a church already in existence there. Nehemiah Machakaire accepted the invitation to join The Methodist Episcopal Church, and was subsequently appointed to take charge of the Muziti congregation. It is interesting to note that, to this day, Muziti has remained one of the strongest rural congregations of the Zimbabwe Annual Conference.

The expansion of The Methodist Episcopal Church in the first decade of the twentieth century was accompanied by efforts to train African leadership. At the fourth session of the East Central African Mission Conference it was decided that courses of study for African leaders designated "native courses for study for Rhodesia Central Africa Mission Conference" should be introduced. These courses were divided into two main areas of study, namely courses for teachers and courses for local preachers. In both cases the duration of the courses was four years. The introduction of such studies was significant in that it recognized the importance of leadership training in the life of the Church. Another important development was that for the first time the "native workers" were listed in the official records of The Methodist Episcopal Church.

In his drive to expand the activities of The Methodist Episcopal Church to cover eastern Southern Rhodesia and Northern Rhodesia, Bishop Hartzell made proposals to the British South African Company in 1905 to exchange land at Old Mutare for an equivalent amount of land in the above-mentioned two places. In a carefully worded letter to the British South Africa Company, Bishop Hartzell justified his proposal for a quid pro quo of land:

> In my last interview with Mr. Rhodes we planned largely for the Mission as a whole, and he gave assurance of co-operation as

needed from himself and friends. Since then, several important changes have occurred. It is evident that stock raising cannot be undertaken safely on a large scale until the cattle-disease is wholly extirpated from the country. A large part of the Mission Estate as it is now cannot be utilized except in stock-raising. Much of it lies in the midst of gold mining centers which are growing in number and activity, and all mining rights were reserved. Other sections of the estate which we cannot use now are well adapted to farming, and could be utilized by the Government in its plans to bring into the country new settlers. My feeling is that after retaining ample land for the use of the Mission, the larger interests of Rhodesia, which concern us all, suggest that the remainder of the estate should be open to public use as the Government may direct.

My proposition to the Government is as follows: What is known as the Old Town site contains about 500 morgen [1 morgen = 2.116 acres or 0.856 hectare]. Here our buildings and most of our farm developments are located. To this we have title in fee simple. Adjoining this is 100 morgen which we bought, and to which we also have full title. We will need an additional adjoining tract of about 400 or 500 morgen to enable us to have irrigation on some part of our land. Water cannot be brought on any part of the Old Town site. This would give the Mission about 800 or 1000 morgen: the exact area to be determined by the final survey. This is enough for many years' growth, as we cannot carry out the original plan of cattle raising. This leaves 500 or more morgen which I propose to return to the Government on condition that the same amount of land be granted elsewhere for Mission purposes in Southern or Northern Rhodesia in such places and amounts as may be mutually agreed upon. As we bore the expense of survey and transfer to ourselves, the Government should bear the expense of survey and re-transfer of the 500 morgen.[7]

In its reply, the British South Africa Company expressed its willingness to grant the same amount of land "elsewhere for mission purposes in Southern Rhodesia in such places and extends as may be mutually agreed upon, provided as regards Northern Rhodesia that the concurrence of the Board [of Directors of the British South Africa Company] which has been telegraphed is obtained."[8] The board of directors subsequently approved the arrangement but then negotiations to acquire land in Northern Rhodesia for missionary work by The Methodist Episcopal Church in exchange for the part of Old Mutare land to be given back to government did not materialize. Most likely, the failure of The Methodist Episcopal

Church to establish mission stations in the Zambezi River region had to do with the comity arrangement among missionary groups. As a matter of fact, The Methodist Episcopal Church reached a gentleman's agreement with the Salvation Army who had been working in the Zambezi area for some time. This was the case in Masvingo where the work that had been started by Johannes Chimene in the then Fort Victoria area was later on forfeited by The Methodist Episcopal Church to the Dutch Reformed Church in the area. These agreements were reached at the sessions of the Rhodesia Missionary Conference.

Expansion Toward the Zambezi River

However, while these discussions were taking place, some Methodist Episcopal Church missionaries were busy exploring the Zambezi area for missionary work. In this respect, two missionaries in particular, Springer and Coffin, deserve mention.

The extension of missionary activities into Murewa was largely the work of John M. Springer. Between June 1905 and October 1906 he visited Murewa several times, initially alone, but later with Coffin. He found Murewa "densely populated" by the local Africans, foreign traders, and government officials. He described the Murewa people as "friendly but shy." The next target of his missionary activities was Mutoko, forty miles to the east of Murewa. His impression was that there was "a good opening for a mission station." He described the people as "very wild usually running for the veld on the approach of a white person." Springer and Coffin "continued on north and a little west through Mt. Darwin . . . to the Zambezi River." The main purpose of these explorations was to establish at least seven main stations, namely Murewa, Mutoko, Katerere, Nyanga, Cabora Bassa, Sena, and Gorongoza. "From these centers," wrote Springer, "outstations should increase until the whole district is covered." These efforts were intended to extend the boundaries of The Methodist Episcopal Church work from Old Umtali to the Zambezi. A district with the name "The Zambezi District" was even created; but as noted earlier, with the exception of Murewa and Mutoko, which have remained strongholds of Methodism, the northward thrust toward the Zambezi did not yield enduring results. The explorations made by Springer and Coffin were followed by practical steps to create and consolidate a circuit of The Methodist Episcopal Church in both Murewa and Mutoko. In 1909 Samuel Gurney was put in charge of the Murewa station with the assistance of one "native helper," and by 1910 two other missionaries with "native helpers" had been appointed to work at Murewa, namely Edward McLean, John Potter, and James Apiri.

By the time of the conference of 1911, two more people had been appointed to serve at Murewa, namely James Marimeta at Marimeta and Job Tsiga. Edward McLean had been transferred to Mutoko. By 1912 James Apiri had also been transferred to Mutoko, most probably the first African evangelist to be appointed there. He was succeeded by Isaiah Kashayanyama (Munjoma) in 1915. It is noteworthy that by 1915 the circuit was no longer just Murewa with Mutoko listed as a station; rather it was known as Murewa and Mutoko Circuit, a clear indication that church work in Mutoko was progressing well.

All along, the East Central Africa Mission Conference consisted of two districts: Inhambane and Mutare Districts. Because of the zeal by missionaries in Rhodesia which had originally been shown by Bishop Hartzell as he tried to acquire more land across the Zambezi in Northern Rhodesia by action of the 1910 conference, the Mutare District was split into two districts called the Mutare and the Zambezi Districts. As already mentioned, negotiations to acquire land in Northern Rhodesia for missionary work by The Methodist Episcopal Church in exchange for the part of Old Mutare land did not materialize. Most likely, the second reason, which affected the development of Methodist mission stations in the Zambezi River, was the comity arrangement among missionary groups. Hence, by action of the tenth session of the East Central Africa Mission Conference in 1913, the two districts of Mutare and Zambezi were merged once more, forming the Rhodesia District.

The Enabling Act of the General Conference of 1912 allowed the division of the East Central Africa Mission Conference into two mission conferences, the Rhodesian Mission Conference and the Portuguese East Africa Mission Conference. As far as the work of The Methodist Episcopal Church was concerned, the last session of the East Central Africa Mission Conference was held in 1915, while the year 1916 marked the first session of the Rhodesia Mission Conference.

Summary

(1) African leaders were present as participants at the first session of the East Central Africa Mission Conference in Mutare, in 1901. They were Tizore Navess of Southeast Africa and Charles Yafele of Rhodesia. George Muponda was recorded as a teacher in Mutare.

(2) While names of missionaries were often recorded whenever they were involved in missionary activities even at that early period of the establishment of The Methodist Episcopal Church, that was not always the case with African leaders. Often African leaders were referred to merely as "native evangelists," "native assistants," and so forth.

(3) The pattern of church growth and expansion during those early days is also significant. Initially, a missionary would approach a chief; the chief would ask for a school or a teacher; and the pastor-teacher or evangelist was then sent to the chief's village or area to start work.

(4) Mutare and Old Mutare became bases from which United Methodist expansion took place both to the southern and northern parts of the country.

(5) While it is true that Bishop Hartzell and fellow American missionaries introduced The Methodist Episcopal Church in Rhodesia, these early missionaries found two African evangelists— Johannes Chimene and Nehemiah Machakaire—already preaching and evangelizing their own people without the support of any missionary societies. That can be viewed as proof that if missionaries had not come to Rhodesia at the time they did, African initiative in the preaching of the gospel could still have taken place.

(6) All Methodist Episcopal Church work from 1901 to 1909 was carried out under the auspices of the Mutare District. From 1910 to 1912 there were two districts, namely the Mutare and Zambezi Districts; and from 1913 to 1915 the two districts merged to form the Rhodesia District again.

(7) Further, we note the termination of the East Central Africa Mission Conference when, by action of the 1912 General Conference, two mission conferences were formed in 1915; namely the Rhodesia Mission Conference and the Portuguese East Africa Mission Conference.

(8) It is important to emphasize that African leaders labored

side by side with white missionaries in pioneering the establishment of The Methodist Episcopal Church in Rhodesia; namely Charles Yafele, George Muponda, John Malgas, William Yafele, and David Ntuli in the Mutare, Penhalonga, and Muradzikwa areas; Stephen Tiki and John Mazonya were the first bishop's appointees in Chief Mutambara's area, David Mandisodza in Chief Marange's area, and John Potter, James Apiri, James Marimeta, and Job Tamutsa in the Murewa and Mutoko areas.

(9) Bishop Hartzell's desire to establish a mission in Northern Rhodesia and efforts by several missionaries to extend boundaries to the Zambezi River have recently been fulfilled. Today, the Zimbabwe Annual Conference of The United Methodist Church boasts of church work in Zambia and Malawi, including a district in South Africa.

Part II

The Church as an Institution (1921–1945)

During this period, The Methodist Episcopal Church emerged more as an institution than it had during the earlier period. The Methodist Episcopal Church had to be modelled both ecclesiastically and theologically. The adaption and application of institutional organizations and regulations of the Church were introduced vigorously to the new Church as we shall read in the following three chapters.

Chapter 5

Church Identity and Solidification

During the early days of the life of The Methodist Episcopal Church in Southern Rhodesia, the tasks of evangelism and education were not easily distinguishable. In the years 1921–1945, however, The Methodist Episcopal Church saw the need to strengthen the Christian faith of believers and to instruct members in their understanding of Methodism. Three elements contributed to this new situation: the revival of 1918, camp meetings and class meetings, and church leadership.

The Revival of 1918

The 1918 revival stands out as the beginning of a new era in the life of The United Methodist Church, even to many Christians who are still alive. Indeed, my own parents trace the origin of their Christian life back to 1918.

A brief historical account of the revival will help us understand what was involved. Some oral sources say that it all began with a girl at Rusitu, a mission station of the American Board of Commissioners for Foreign Missions of the Congregational Christian Churches, south of Mutare, who triggered the events with a testimony that she gave. The documents, however, start with Reverend James Hatch, a congregational missionary at Rusitu, who came to Old Mutare with some other Christians in June 1918. All pastor-teachers had been invited to Old Mutare to the first camp meeting of The Methodist Episcopal Church in Southern Rhodesia then. In an afternoon service Hatch preached, telling people the wonderful things God had revealed to his people at Rusitu and the way the Holy Spirit had come upon them. Those who had come with Hatch witnessed to the same events. But some of the Old Mutare people laughed at their visitors, calling them false prophets. Late in the afternoon of that day, when Hatch was preaching again, the church is said to have been filled with various noises from people. The reporter goes on to say: "That day our Methodist Church was filled with the Holy Spirit and it became clear in our minds that Reverend Hatch had really said what he had perceived."[1]

While some people went to bed, others stayed in the church, and throughout the night incessant praying and shouting went on. Following the meeting, pastor-teachers were sent out in the villages to preach the Holy Spirit, and many people were converted to Christianity. As the pastor-teachers went from Old Mutare back to their different homes, all the mission centers and many other village churches were shaken with a fresh spiritual fervor. John Gates' report emphasized the revival's effect upon the African people. John Paisley, a missionary at Nyakatsapa, goes a step further and commented on his own family's deep involvement. Reporting on the well-frequented July quarterly meeting at Nyakatsapa Mission, Paisley wrote:

> From the very first meeting it was evident that the Spirit of the Lord was at work, but not until the third day came the direct manifestation of a real Pentecost. Such a scene my wife and I will never forget, and is best described in the second chapter of Acts.[2]

Paisley reported a great crowd for the October quarterly meeting, the largest gathering they had ever had for this kind of meeting, with many people coming for baptism. He attributed it to the obedience of many people and to the evangelists who had worked hard, going from one village to another as they responded to the prompting of the Holy Spirit.

The revival had its miracles, too. There were manifestations of the glory of Christ that people believed to be the work of God himself. There is one miracle in particular almost every member of The United Methodist Church in Zimbabwe must have heard about in one way or another. The story goes like this: Nhenhu Muredzwa, a daughter of *Ishe* (chieftess) Muredzwa of Zinyembe, was about six years old when her hands and legs became deformed. The cause of the deformity was not known, despite all the consultation of diviners. Nhenhu spent her days lying down and had to be carried everywhere. Some of the African pastor-teachers—John Cheke, David Mandisodza, Gezana Sadomba, and others who were at Old Mutare when the revival broke out—came to Nyakatsapa Circuit (of which Zinyembe, Nhenhu's area or village was part) preaching the gospel. Naturally, everyone began to talk about the preachers in the area. When the preachers entered Zinyembe village, Nhenhu wanted to see and hear them for herself.

After obtaining permission from the Chieftess Muredzwa, the preachers went to the house where Nhenhu lived. After a season of prayer, Gezana Sadomba got up and held Nhenhu from her armpits, with David Mandisodza laying his hands on her head, and while everyone was in the spirit of prayer and great expectation, John Cheke repeated the Apostle's words, "In the name of Jesus Christ of Nazareth, walk" (Acts 3:6). As they lifted her, Nhenhu stood on her feet and began to walk. In describing the impact of the miracle, John Paisley said "the whole country around was stirred to its depth." Nhenhu, who was baptized, became known as Dorcas. She is said to have been a faithful member of The United Methodist Church until her death in July 1972.[3]

What did the 1918 revival mean to The Methodist Episcopal Church in Southern Rhodesia? There are three things that stand out in the reports about this revival that are of significance to the life of United Methodism in Zimbabwe to this day. First, J. Machiwenyika's interpretation of the people receiving the Holy Spirit at Old Mutare sees the Spirit being given to the Church, and not to people as individuals. This is the way in which he witnessed the event:

> During his preaching, some people began fainting, others crying and others saying that they were inspired with the Holy Spirit. The Church was filled with various noises from various people. That day, our Methodist Church was filled with the Holy Spirit and it became clear in our minds that Reverend Hatch had really said what he had perceived.[4]

In other words, what was happening to individuals was something that was happening to the church. It occurred to the people because they belonged to the church. I can confirm this from my own observations of the elderly church members who were part of the 1918 revival. They always talk of "our church" as the Church of the Holy Spirit; very rarely is the Holy Spirit of 1918 claimed by individual people.

Second, the 1918 revival in the life of Church may well stand out as the work of the Holy Spirit, if the Holy Spirit can be credited with striving to liberate the twenty-one-year-old Church from being mission-stationed, while remaining Westernized in the African situation. Only when Christianity was willing to become African-ized, or incarnate in the African life, did it become appealing. And that was precisely what the revival of 1918 did in The Methodist Episcopal Church. No wonder that, while many missionaries did not look at it favorably, Africans greatly rejoiced in it. In spite of positive results in the work of the larger Church, some missionaries perceived the revival as detrimental to the African people. Except for a few missionaries like Paisley, most did not report much about what the revival did to them. In the report, "The State of the Church," prepared by three missionaries, this much was said:

> Last June there came upon our native teachers a baptism—a Pentecost. We are not impressed with the gymnastics that some went through, but a large number of our men became flaming fires with a heavy burden for their people rolled upon them.[5]

It might be more correct, however, to say that missionaries were more concerned with the dominance of emotions over intellect in the way people expressed their religious faith during the revival. Also, it could be said that the lack of interest and acquaintance with the traditional religious life of African people on the part of the missionaries could have been a determining factor in their uneasy attitude about the revival. Nevertheless, the revival set the Church on a different path—a path more familiar to African Christians. There they met their Master, and in the best way they knew how, they ran swiftly to meet God in Christ Jesus, revealed by the power of the Holy Spirit. If the missionary who had prayed for spiritual renewal expected Christ Jesus to come to the African on Western terms and for the African to respond in Western ways, he or she was disappointed.

The 1918 revival was one of those occasions when the Holy Spirit seemed to hustle the Church from missionary hands into contextual forms of African life. It was like a dam of water that had burst its walls, leaving the water free to take its natural course. Thus, Christianity, through the power of the Holy Spirit, could find its way into African life as a new faith. As preachers and groups went from one village to another, for the first time people began to hear the gospel clearly and distinctly in their own language and style. Indigenization of the gospel is always another Pentecost because it gives people the opportunity to hear the good news in their own cultural language and to perceive the Christian faith in relation to their own style and pattern of life.

Third, for many people in Zimbabwe, particularly the elderly people and those who still think in terms of revival events, 1918 represents the real beginning of United Methodism. They do not seem to care what went on before that revival. If they do, it does not seem important because it really did not affect them as the revival had. The revival had results. Many people were converted; new out-stations were opened and many young people presented themselves for the ministry. There were many results to cite from the revival. Yet, the crucial issue of the revival which still grips people today is that it was one of those brief periods when the Church was truly African. The Church was "turned upside down" to use Luke's words (Acts 17:6), or "inside out," to use Hoekendijk's formulation. What a tragedy, then, that the trend after the 1918 revival was to turn the Church back to the mission station again, back into the hands of those who tended to perceive the Church in terms of Western ways of life, missionaries and Africans alike.

Camp Meetings and Class Meetings

Eight years after the 1918 revival, the Conference Committee on Evangelism argued that the ground that was gained by the revival meetings was going to be lost entirely if the Church was not prepared to do something about it. The new converts who needed constant contact with the Church for growth in their Christian faith and understanding of the Christian life were a challenge. The warning of the Committee on Evangelism was quite in order, for if the revival had not prepared the officials of The Methodist Episcopal Church for a new era, it had certainly done so for the people. This was illustrated in 1932 when Johane Marange, a local preacher in the Methodist Episcopal Church, was disciplined by the Church; he then broke away with several members. The challenge that Johane Marange brought to The Methodist Episcopal Church was manifold. He baptized his converts immediately upon their confession of Christ, without any probationary period, and he claimed to have "a free, no-collection church," very unlike the practice in The Methodist Episcopal Church then. Visions and dreams found a place in his new movement, while in his former church it was never clear whether they had any place or not. This opened the eyes of The Methodist Episcopal Church to the need for an ongoing Christian education program, as well as continuing evangelistic work. During this time camp meetings became the most prominent method of evangelism, while class meetings became the preferred way of teaching people the Christian faith.

Camp Meetings

We have already noted the first camp meeting at Old Mutare on 4 June 1918 to which only the pastor-teachers were invited. However, it was not until 1928 that camp meetings were promoted on a grand scale through the efforts of Marshall J. Murphree, who started the Nyatande Camp Meeting near Gandanzara. Over a thousand people are reported to have attended the first Nyatande Camp Meeting, representing about twenty stations during the closing Sunday service. By the 1930s, camp meetings had become the most popular way to bring many people together. Favorable reports came from all over, according to Jackson Rugayo from Mutambara, who in 1936 reported "the camp meetings in Southern Rhodesia are bringing a great religious harvest," in evangelistic outreach and in strengthening the faith of Christians.

Camp meetings recaptured the spirit of 1918 as people invoked the power of the Holy Spirit. Yet there was one striking difference. The 1918 revival was centered on the local church; camp meetings were not. The revival enabled people to work on the scene—within the local church structure, either by having preachers come in or by one congregation going elsewhere. This strengthened local churches in their evangelistic task in villages that surrounded them. Camp meetings, however, although they also had a tremendous impact, unfortunately pulled people out of their local situation. A tendency arose to go to camp meetings for their own sake or for one's own religious needs, rather than for the evangelization of nonbelievers. M. J. Murphree observed:

> Since coming to Africa I have often thought Camp Meetings, after the manner of some which I have attended in the homeland, would be of great power and influence among our people here.[6]

Camp meetings were indeed conducted in the manner in which

they had been imported from America and thus never became sufficiently Africanized.

The leadership of camp meetings remained missionary-centered. As thousands of people gathered at camp meetings technical problems had to be faced, namely public sound systems, sufficient lighting for the evening services, and so on. Administratively, some kind of a schedule had to be made and enforced with time for services and time for eating. Though African ministers were involved in the preaching program of camp meetings, in order for the total program to function there had to be a missionary behind it all—someone who had the skills necessary for organizing people in mass meetings.

Class Meetings

The Methodist Episcopal Church in Southern Rhodesia, then, always emphasized the use of class meetings as a vital tradition of Methodism. As elsewhere, so also in Africa the spirit of the class meetings and their educational thrust informed the goals of the Sunday schools, a movement not originally Methodist in character. However, during the 1920s what was true of class meetings was also true of Sunday school in the country. Together they were the means of trying to help the Church understand its faith.

According to "An All-South Africa Program and Policy" report, missionary societies working in Africa (south of the equator) in the 1920s were operating under a dual crisis. The first problem was the "determination of the African to break with paganism and embrace a new life in a new world."[7] Certainly this was an interpretation of missionaries about the success of their work in Africa, which led them to the speculation that the African was abandoning all his past to embrace the new. Second, it was believed that the Moslems were determined to thrust their religion upon the whole of Africa. This view was very strong among the missionaries. According to the report, as early as 1917 Moslems were known to be gaining about forty thousand adherents annually. In addition, missionaries already suspected that the situation in Africa was also ripe for Ethiopianism. The notion of "Ethiopianism" was defined recently by Bishop Bengt Sundkler in his study of independent Bantu churches in which he distinguished between two main types of African independent churches: the "Ethiopians" and the "Zionist" churches. Sundkler defines "Ethiopians" as those independent Bantu churches that have "(a) seceded from White Mission churches chiefly on racial grounds, or (b) other Bantu churches seceding from the Bantu leaders classified under (a)."[8] Although this type of church is against white domination, their church organization and biblical interpretation largely follows the patterns of churches from which they seceded. Another type is that of the "Zionists" which are now "a syncretistic Bantu movement with healing, speaking in tongues, purification rites and taboos as the main expression of their faith."[9]

Historically, the Zionists (according to Sundkler) have their roots in Zion City, Illinois, USA. It is very possible that the use of the term "Ethiopianism" by missionaries in Africa in the 1920s was inclusive of all independent Bantu churches. And if we consider that there are thousands of distinct religious movements in sub-Saharan Africa today, then we can see how justifiable missionary fears were in the 1920s.

Islam was considered a worse enemy than Ethiopianism. Even into the 1950s, it was not uncommon to hear missionaries and some of the African ministers say that nine out of every ten converts in Africa were won to Islam. The fear of Islam was shared by all missionary societies south of the equator. Yet The Methodist Episcopal Church in Southern Rhodesia, like many other churches in that part of Africa, was probably more afraid of Ethiopianism than Islam. We have already noted how Johane Marange broke away with a number of followers from The Methodist Episcopal Church. The emergence of independent churches in Africa revealed the importance of Christian education. Thus, class meetings became an important means of helping Christians understand their faith.

Class meetings tended to have two roles. Their first role was educational in a broad sense. Class meetings became a way of keeping in touch with all members of the Church in accordance with the Methodist tradition. People were divided into groups of twelve with a leader. In these groups new people were taught how to pray and were assured of the fact that the group cared for them. The second role of class meetings was more strictly educational. Probationers were expected to spend a period of two years in learning the new faith. The Lord's Prayer and the Apostle's Creed had to be committed to memory. Furthermore, doctrines of the Church and rule of The Methodist Episcopal Church as laid down in the *Discipline* had to be studied. New members also learned many other things, such as the Catechism, Christian hymns, and the new style of Christian life. Therefore, class meetings met a real need although in the course of time, like many other unchanged methods, they lost part of their effectiveness.

The Rise of an Indigenous Ordained Ministry

The first African minister to be ordained a deacon in The Methodist Episcopal Church in Southern Rhodesia was David Mandisodza in 1921. In 1929 Clifford Faku, Reginald Ngonyama, Thomas Marange, and David Mandisodza were the first to be ordained elders. These events signalled a new era, a new chapter in the history of The Methodist Episcopal Church. African leaders were moving into areas and positions of the conference where decisions were made.

A training school was started at Old Mutare in 1919, with three departments: theological, literary and normal, and industrial. In 1929, the department of theology pulled out of the training school to establish itself separately as a theological school, with seven full-time students and four who were part-time, since they were also involved in the training school. In 1934 and 1935 the theological school also had two students from the Zaire Mission Conference and one from the American Board of Foreign Missions. The school had its hard days; it was closed from 1936 to 1938. After opening its doors again in 1939, it never again closed.

What was the conception of the ministry, then, for which The Methodist Episcopal Church in Southern Rhodesia trained Africans for ordination? For an easy answer one could, of course, refer to *The Book of Discipline of the United Methodist Church*, and to *The Discipline of the Central Africa Conference*. This would, however, not answer our concern for a ministry of The Methodist Episcopal Church in Southern Rhodesia in relation to the African experience. Unfortunately no coherent expositions on this subject are extant. Nevertheless, we have enough material to help us understand what must have been fundamental to the vision. Two factors clearly stand out: the need for an indigenous ordained ministry and a conception of ministry.

An Indigenous Ordained Ministry

First, the revival of 1918 revealed the urgent need for the African ordained ministry in The Methodist Episcopal Church. (1) As John Gates pointed out in his report to conference in 1919, out-stations were opened at the rate of about one every month and some of the stations that had been closed subsequently reopened. Consequently, these various stations required ministers. (2) Practically every mission station in the conference reported an increase in church attendance, Sunday school, and class meetings. Thus, more ministers were needed. (3) Over forty young Africans volunteered for Christian service. Here was the promise of an answer to the need for an indigenous ordained ministry.

Second, there existed a growing and irritating problem of the adequate administration of the sacraments to the growing membership of Methodism in Southern Rhodesia: (1) In the face of groups breaking away in the 1930s the need to teach the meaning of and to prepare people for Christian baptism became crucial; and (2) the infrequency with which members of The Methodist Episcopal Church received the Lord's Supper was disturbing. Many waited until the quarterly meeting when the district superintendent and a few ordained African ministers would be available to administer sacraments; this aroused a feeling of dissatisfaction in the Church. For some time there had been a confusion in the conference regarding the lack of uniformity in the administering or denying of the sacrament of the Lord's Supper to probationers. Naturally this created problems that pastor-teachers could not solve. A church that does not meet its sacramental responsibilities in Africa, particularly with baptism, is vulnerable to independent African churches and runs the risk of an independent group breaking away from it.

Third, the breakaway of Johane Marange in 1932 with a considerable number of Methodists following him in the Marange area, one of the strongholds of The United Methodist Church to this day, heightened the fear of strange doctrines in the conference. Consequently, in a 1933 "State of the Church" report, church leaders were called upon to do everything within their power to lead their people into a deeper spiritual life. It can be seen that all of these factors, and probably many others not known to us, contributed to the rise of an indigenous ordained ministry in The Methodist Episcopal Church in Southern Rhodesia.

The Conception of Ministry

In order to understand the conception of ministry that The Methodist Episcopal Church in Southern Rhodesia then espoused, we turn to the manner or style in which Africans were trained for ordination. First, ministerial training was person-centered. A ministerial candidate had to meet certain qualifications. (1) The candidate's spirituality was crucially important, as the Committee on Evangelism reported to the conference in 1919:

> Spiritually, no pastor-teacher or evangelist should be sent out, no matter what educational qualifications he may possess, without giving evidence of a definite conversion.[10]

This statement was meant for pastor-teachers because there were no Africans ordained at that point. Yet when the latter appeared on the scene, the statement still remained true. The statement of a genuine conversion experience is still required of all candidates by the Board of Ordained Ministry. Conversion experience was seen as the springboard from which "a burden for salvation of the people . . . a life of prayer" emerged. In connection with or in addition to the conversion experience, a ministerial candidate was then expected to point to a specific call by God to preach the gospel.

(2) The candidate's educational qualifications: Although spiritual qualifications seemed more important than academic ones, the latter were not unimportant. Marshall J. Murphree, who was responsible for theological training in the conference from the 1930s through the 1940s, pointed out that the purpose of theological training was to deepen the spiritual life of every student, "as well as the acquirement of knowledge." But the educational qualifications for those who were to train for the ministry in The Methodist Episcopal Church included an ability to teach the people how to make better gardens and how to erect a simple house of brick and to make simple furniture. While one may disagree with some of the details, the message is clear that theological training is meant to enable the minister to help his people in both spiritual and temporal things.

Second, ministry in The Methodist Episcopal Church in Southern Rhodesia was biblically-oriented. (1) The intensity with which the Bible is mentioned and the central place to which it is assigned, both in theological training and in the ministry itself, is worth noticing as one reads through the journals. (2) Continuing education: A considerable number of educational programs were designed for the pastor-teachers who were already working in the circuits. Again, these were mainly biblical courses which included devotions, Bible study, and memorizing Scripture. The courses were instructed by Greeley, who also taught hymn singing. Similarly, several programs of a "Bible Training Course" were planned at the conference level for pastor-teachers and those aspiring for ordination.

Our sources are silent on how the Bible was interpreted. All we can say with confidence is that the Bible was central in the ministry of The Methodist Episcopal Church. Clearly the chief goals were providing the minister with biblical knowledge as a means of closer communion with God, and enabling him as a preacher to "learn how to 'rightly' divide the Word," whatever may have been included in this formulation.

Third, ministry in The Methodist Episcopal Church in Southern Rhodesia was evangelistically tempered. This began with missionaries, as John Gates said:

> Our task as Christian workers is to evangelize Africa. . . . Our native workers are pastor-teachers, not teacher-pastors. Evangelism comes first. Education without religion is worse than heathenism.[11]

Evangelism was put above everything else. Naturally, missionaries instilled the same obligation in the emerging indigenous ordained ministry in at least two ways: (1) A course on the study of evangelism was taught in the theological school and "augmented by the practical experience gained in the camp meetings." With impressive frequency, practical work for seminarians was associated with camp meetings and other occasions that provided the opportunity for evangelistic training. One is tempted to think that probably evangelism was the only practical program ministerial students had. (2) Similarly, special courses in evangelism were organized for those who were already in circuits. The ministry of Christ Jesus in The Methodist Episcopal Church was related to the African experience in Southern Rhodesia, first by an emphasis on a conversion experience and a personal call from God into the ministry; and second, by an emphasis on the biblical knowledge of

78

the saving acts of God, with the intent to share that saving knowledge with the rest of the world.

Summary

(1) There was a sense in which some Africans interpreted the revival of 1918 as a providential effort by the Holy Spirit to liberate the Church from the hands of Western control so as to contextualize it.

(2) The missionaries' response through the mission conference was to place more emphasis on class meetings, Sunday school, camp meetings, and the corresponding training of an indigenous ordained ministry.

(3) At the outset, Methodist theological orientation was introduced and emphasized in the training and rising of African indigenous ordained ministry; namely, that it was person-centered, biblically-oriented, and evangelistic in disposition.

Chapter 6

Christianity Confronting African Culture

When Methodist Episcopal Church missionaries came to Southern Rhodesia they brought with them not only the Christian gospel, but also the culture in which the gospel was embodied for them. In addition to the Good News, missionaries introduced their Western modes of worship and these became the "true" Christian way of adoration. They applied what they believed to be the Christian way of life to many areas of African life without much awareness of the African culture that they addressed. Specifically in this chapter we will examine three areas of The Methodist Episcopal Church's teaching in Southern Rhodesia: African patterns and practices of marriage, community and social life; and African traditional religion.

African Patterns and Practices of Marriage

Marriage is one area of the Christian life where a new theology is urgently needed. Many rules and regulations were introduced by successive conferences of The United Methodist Church, particularly for the African Christians during the years 1921–25. Polygamy was attacked at the very first session of the East Central Africa Mission Conference in 1901. The conference followed the action of Erwin Richards, who, at the Inhambane Mission, refused membership in the Church to persons with more than one wife. Richards had been in Southeast Africa since 1880 with the American Board Mission; his action set the precedent for the new Church.

Reasons for the practice of polygamy differ from one region to another in Africa. However, the 1963 All-African Seminar on Christian Home and Family Life agreed on the following three basic reasons: custom, sterility of the first wife, and provision for a sick wife.[1]

Custom

Among the Shona people of Zimbabwe, as with other ethnic groups, the taking of a deceased brother's wife is usually a family decision, and that decision is made ceremonially. It is customary among the Shona people that after a person is dead and buried a day is set on which to divide his belongings among relatives. In the case of a man who has left a widow, consideration is given to her needs. Under normal circumstances she is the one who should make the decision whether she wants to take as a husband a brother of her deceased husband.

The way the decision is made is that, after all the belongings of her deceased husband have been divided among relatives, the sister of the deceased sits down on a mat. The widow comes to sit next to her. Ceremonial weapons, like a bow and arrow, an axe, or a spear of the deceased husband are presented to the sister of the deceased, who immediately passes them on to the widow sitting next to her. The widow has three options in declaring her wishes in front of her family and that of her deceased husband, and all the relatives. First, if she had a son, she would turn to her son and hand over the weapons to him. In so doing, she symbolically recognizes the fact that her husband is now dead, and the son he left must now fend for her needs. Thus, she acknowledges that her son will look after her, and declares that she does not want the brothers of the deceased to bother her.

Second, after receiving the weapons from the sister of the deceased, she could return those weapons to the sister of the deceased again. That could be done if the deceased husband left daughters but no son, for the weapons would never be passed on to a daughter. It could also be done by a widow who was left without a child. However, returning the weapons to the sister of the deceased symbolically means that the widow is going to stay with the family or clan, but has no intention of taking one of her deceased husband's brothers as her husband. In another way, she is saying to the sister of the deceased, "You will look after me as long as I continue staying within the family."

Third, in the case of a widow who wishes to marry a brother of her deceased husband, after receiving the weapons from the sister of the deceased man, she would stand up with the weapons given to her in the presence of the two families and relatives, go to the brother of the deceased, kneel before him, and hand over the weapons to him. This action signifies that the brother is her new husband.

There are two points to be clarified. Among the Shona people, the emphasis of that kind of marriage was to look after the children that already existed, rather than just taking another wife. It was a way of ensuring that children always have two parents and also of acknowledging that every adult needs companionship. The two families would first have discussed matters to discern the wishes of the widow so that no one would be taken by surprise. If the widow opted to be a wife to one of the brothers who was already married, the sisters would discuss the issue with the wife of that brother to make sure that she accepted the arrangement.

Sterility or Illness of the First Wife

Another reason for the practice of polygamy centers around the role of children. In rural society, children literally were necessary for the daily survival of families, as well as important to ancestral survival through them. The continuation of the family name was essential.

I once served as a pastor in an area where the custom was that if a wife realized she was sickly and had a feeling that she might die soon, she would arrange for either her own sister or a close relative to be married by her husband as a second wife. Then if she died, her children were not left to be taken care of by a strange woman. It was in effect a security plan for the children.

This is not the place to debate the advantages and disadvantages of polygamy; we read in Genesis 2:24 God's plan for marriage as monogamy. The problem is more specifically what to do with a polygamist, with one who is already in that situation. First, in 1942, the Southern Rhodesia Annual Conference made its position very clear when it stated that "A male polygamist, or the second or subsequent wife, cannot be baptized or received into the membership of the Church."[2]

The problem with this position taken by The Methodist Church is that it makes a polygamist a special sinner, the only one who is not permitted to join the Church. Such a position forces a polygamist either to give up his Christian faith or to expel his other wives and children, which could be socially disastrous. This is the position that The United Methodist Church in Zimbabwe still holds to this day.

Second, in 1925 the Southern Rhodesia Mission Conference of The Methodist Episcopal Church passed a ruling against *kuroodza*—parents choosing a marriage partner for their daughter or son. In a number of African countries, the two prevalent practices of choosing a partner were as follows: (1) Parents or the extended family chose the future spouse for their children when they reached puberty or, at times, even while the child was still in the mother's womb. (2) The parents or the extended family waited until their son told them which girl he wanted to marry and the family would approach the family of the girl. It would then be up to the girl's family to approach their daughter and present the proposal. Here it should be noted also that the parents or extended family who had a daughter whom they wished to be married into a particular family also had the liberty to take the first move in approaching that family on their daughter's behalf. Although it was the first of the two practices which aroused the Church's particular opposition, both practices were really considered inadequate according to Western culture in light of the romantic argument that the two people had no opportunity to know each other.

For Africans however, both of these practices have something worth preserving: the fact that marriage is an arrangement between two families and not just an affair of the two individuals. The involvement of families in the marriage of two people is consistent with African customary life, where no person or persons can set themselves apart from the rest of the family. In African eyes, the fear of intruding in-laws is the problem of Western marriages. Africa has something to offer in the recognition of the existence of the two families, for is it not also Christian to understand marriage in the context of community life? It is in the community that we all find stability and renewal of life, through being involved in each other's lives.

Third, in 1942 the Southern Rhodesia Annual Conference of The Methodist Church made a statement in connection with the burning issue of *lobola*, very often known as "bride's price" (the term "bride's price" is used here for lack of a better one):

> We recognize that *lobola* is an integral part of the Bantu social custom and consider that its true purpose should be to act as a

token and pledge of care and proper conduct. We urge our members to discourage the present practice of excessive payments.[3]

In this case, it has proven helpful to look at the problem in its historical setting. *Lobola* originated as a sign of friendship or new relationship between two families. Among the Shona, oral tradition in some areas informs us that the future son-in-law always presented something to his future in-laws to demonstrate that he had acquired some skills and that he was a man in society. Many men fulfilled this requirement through services like building a house for the future in-laws, or by clearing the forest where the in-laws intended to start cultivating. In a time when iron tools were increasingly available, young men were expected to learn the skills of a blacksmith. Thus, one of the precious presentations that a young man could make to his in-laws was a *badza*, an iron hoe. This is the reason why, in some areas, among the Shona people *badza* is a technical term for *lobola*. However, the point is that *lobola* originated as a token of a new friendship or relationship between two families and at the same time as a covenant act of marriage between two individuals. The interpretation of *lobola* as a bride's price has negative connotations, and rightly so. The value of a token is in the event it represents and not necessarily in what one gets out of the thing given, which is the way *lobola* is expressed in a cash economy. On this matter, therefore, The Methodist Church ought to be commended for its insight in upholding a valuable African custom.

Fourth, in 1921 the Southern Rhodesia Mission Conference of The Methodist Episcopal Church ruled against *matorwa*—a boy taking his girlfriend earlier than the time intended. This could mean two things. (1) It could mean that if a girl became pregnant, and the two agreed, the girl would have to leave for her boyfriend's home immediately. (2) It could also mean that after *lobola* was presented according to the African custom, the two were lawfully married in the eyes of society. Should anything prevent their getting together, the two could always arrange for the girl to leave her home.

I resist the interpretation of *matorwa* as elopement, the comparable Western practice, for *matorwa* has had two community sanctions that have to be observed: (1) The girl was not supposed to leave without telling her mother. In fact, she had to tell her mother in time for the mother to help with packing her belongings. But the father was to be left in the dark until the daughter had been gone for a few days. (2) The parents of the boy were expected immediately to send someone to inform the girl's parents that they had their daughter. As long as these rules were observed there was no serious case against the boy. While this was not the best or the normal way of conducting a marriage ceremony, the situation was always normalized with very little difficulty.

Ironically, the Church itself might have increased the problem of *matorwa* by insisting on a "Christian" marriage, i.e. a Westernized marriage, which was too expensive for many young couples. Some young men have had to work two or three years after they had presented their *lobola* in order to have a church marriage that involved buying expensive Western wedding clothes and paying for a big feast. It is in this context that Christian families have experienced the problems of *matorwa*, either because eventually the daughter became pregnant, or the young man was able to engineer a scheme to take away the girl he loved earlier than the parents planned.

Fifth, one of the rules that the Southern Rhodesia Mission Conference passed in 1921 was that Christian men could not allow "inherited women" to live in their homes, even though the plea of caring for them was put forward. By 1942 the rule was that Christian men could not inherit the wives of deceased relatives.[4] The term "inherited women" here is very unfortunate because it lacks understanding of the African custom. If a brother died, the surviving brother was held responsible for taking care of his brother's widow and family. The surviving brother did not have to take his brother's widow as another wife. Such were the difficulties the Church all over Africa experienced as the new faith came into contact with the African culture.

Finally, in 1947 the Southern Rhodesia Annual Conference of The Methodist Church adopted a recommendation from the African Christian Convention (an organization which existed within the Church in Southern Rhodesia composed of African clergymen, laymen, and laywomen, with two missionary advisors) that stated:

This Convention recommends the adoption of the following procedure in conducting backsliders' marriages in our Church:

(a) the bride should not wear a wreath and veil. (b) There should not be any throwing of rice when the couple leaves the church. (c) The marriage ceremony should be conducted in the church.[5]

The last part of the recommendation was an alteration of a strict practice by some ministers who married these kinds of persons either under a tree or in a school classroom instead of using the sanctuary. It should be pointed out that, to many people, Christian marriage was understood in the light of the three points stated above—wearing a wreath and veil, a big party at which people celebrated, and a marriage ceremony in the church. To deprive anyone of these things was understood as a great punishment that the Church used to reprimand those who failed to live up to what was expected of them. Unfortunately, the African understanding of marriage as a union not only of two persons but also of their families is a view that lacks adequate theological consideration of the concept of community around Christ formed by the two families.

African Community and Social Life

In an effort to help African converts adjust in their social life, The Methodist Episcopal Church devised some rules for African Christians. We shall now consider three of these.

First, in 1921 the Southern Rhodesia Mission Conference approved a ruling against Christians participating in nighttime dancing. This is not surprising, for many missionaries understood African dancing, as seen through their Western categories, as erotic in nature. Consequently, the missionaries regarded African nighttime dancing as the work of darkness or heathenism.

Among the Shona people, most villagers spent the whole day in their fields or occupied with other duties. Children, at the time this ruling was made, would be either looking after herds of cattle or working in the fields with their parents. In the evening everyone would be back in the village. When the moon was high and stayed long enough, the people in the villages went dancing—called by the drums. Having grown up in a village setting, I know very well that there was nothing else to do in the evening, especially during or soon after the harvest period. Most young people went out for dancing. The elders would teach the young the difference between clean dances and questionable ones. As young people have always had their heroes, so too these ones would be drawn to those who were extremely good, either in dancing itself or in drum beating. Can you imagine what it meant to Christian families to learn that they were no longer to participate in their traditional dancing?

In 1924 the conference, therefore, found itself requesting missionaries and pastor-teachers to come up with substitute recreational and social activities for Christians. How much of this was done it is hard to say. The only kind of dancing the author recalls while a student at Old Mutare Mission was American folk dancing. That was considered alright. What was accomplished then was to alienate the Africans from their own culture which, however, kept a grip on them. Young people could not be human in the village without participating in dancing. So children from Christian families had to lie to their parents about going out dancing.

Second, in 1921 the Southern Rhodesia Mission Conference warned all pastor-teachers against the use of drinking *mahewu*, an African drink made out of grain. This drink is usually consumed a day after brewing. The weather is a great factor in the process of fermentation, so at times the drink can only be consumed two days later. The light *mahewu* is different from the stronger *doro*, a beer that is consumed a week after brewing. One would find *mahewu* in most African homes that do not condone intoxicating drinks. Even in the homes where *doro* is acceptable most mothers would prepare *mahewu* for children who are prohibited from taking strong drinks.

The prohibition of drinking *mahewu* among Christians in The Methodist Episcopal Church is another example of how the Church in Africa has acted against African cultural life without sufficient knowledge of what was involved. It is indicative of the Church's failure to appreciate African culture and to identify with the African people. Fortunately, the conference reversed its decision on *mahewu* in 1924, although it appended a recommendation that the drink be consumed within twenty-four hours of its brewing.

Third, in 1924 the conference prohibited the use of *doro*. African beer and tobacco were clearly considered evil practices. Tobacco was to be abandoned; a substitute had to be found for beer. Thus, a recommendation was presented to the conference that struck the African, and possibly other people also, as absurd: the village pastor-teachers were to encourage people to plant lemon and orange trees in order to provide a substitute drink for *mahewu* and *doro*. As important as lemons and oranges are for any people, was it not unrealistic to think that fruit drinks would replace traditional drinks? Did lemon and orange juice replace alcoholic beverages in the West? Unfortunately, we do not have any documented sources to inform us of the reactions of the African people regarding the matter in question.

African Traditional Religion

T. A. Beetham made an interesting observation when he said that missionaries who went to China and India were aware that they would necessarily experience a confrontation between their Christian faith and the philosophies of Buddhism and Hinduism. He even went on to point out that those missionaries who earned first-class degrees at Oxford and Cambridge were sent to the East, and in the main, the others were sent to Africa.[6]

The assumption of the Western churches then, like the rest of the Western people, was that Africa was an empty continent, with no history, civilization, or culture of its own. The continent was best known to the Western Christians for what they called heathenism, which actually motivated missionaries to go to Africa. Part of a report by John Gates to the Conference of The Methodist Episcopal Church in Southern Rhodesia in 1919 is illuminating in this regard:

> The people of these pagan lands of Africa are primitive and hopeless. And it seems to us that their primitiveness has hindered them rather than helped them with the Church. If there is a race of people in the world who are represented by the Lazarus in the story of the rich man, or "the one who has been robbed," in the story of the good Samaritan; it is the black man of Africa and his two hundreds of millions of brothers and sisters. Human helplessness is God's loudest language to those to whom He has given wealth and education and power. What a supply other peoples of the world have of life of literature, of history, of at least something beautiful and true in their religious life of philosophy and genius. But all these are absent in Africa.[7]

John Gates was an outstanding and articulate Methodist missionary in his time. He also served as an administrative assistant to Methodist Episcopal Church bishops for Southern Rhodesia, at a time when one bishop was responsible for the administration and pastoral oversight of four conferences in four different countries. Therefore, his statement is representative of the thinking of missionaries about Africa during his time. It reveals the prevalent ignorance about Africa of missionaries who were then working there. They lived in Africa, but they never understood the African culture, let alone the African traditional religion. This is not a judgment on John Gates as a person; after all he was only a child of his age. Certainly it is a judgment upon the whole Church, especially on those who still perpetuate such thinking in Africa today.

It is essential for us today to understand how such an attitude by Western missionaries toward Africa affected the life of the African church. Missionaries felt responsible not only to proclaim the new faith, but also to introduce civilization and culture, meaning Western culture, to Africans. Christianity came from the land and culture of the missionary; the new faith supposedly had nothing to learn from the African cultural context. In order to understand the implications of this attitude, one can look at the following: architectural styles of church buildings, the hymns that African Christians sang in worship, and the substitution of Western and biblical names for those that were authentically African.

When Gezana Sadomba, an unordained African pastor-teacher, presented his report to the conference in 1916 he said that one of the main pastoral problems that he faced in his circuit or parish was the "witch doctors" to whom Christians continued visiting for healing. The practice of going to *n'anga* (herbalist, diviner, or medicine-man), which has been translated "witch doctor" by missionaries, is an institution that has deep roots in the religious and traditional life of the African people. The institution of *n'anga* has not only survived, but actually flourished in our time. Any church that continues viewing *n'anga* as "witch doctor" will be considered as alienating African people from their culture and destroying some of the ingenious native skill and heritage of the African people.

There has been significant amount of interest in African traditional religion lately along with other African areas of study, like anthropology, African history—especially pre-colonial history—sociology, and others. Scholars of African traditional religion have confirmed not only the existence of religious systems among African people, but also a belief in a superhuman Being. Missionaries did not introduce Africans to belief in God. Before Western missionaries ever left their homelands, Africans already knew something about God. The Shona people of Zimbabwe called God by all kinds of names, most of them descriptive of His nature and attributes. For example, the Shona knew Him as Musikavanhu (Creator of people), Nyadenga (He who dwells above), Chidzachepo (He who has always been there), and by many other names. All this knowledge of God came from the pre-Christian era in which missionaries, until recently, have taken no interest.

One would have thought that, if they had been aware of John Wesley's teaching on prevenient grace, Methodist missionaries would not have found this matter a stumbling block. Wesley taught that every individual has a measure of prevenient grace so that no one could claim to have a purely natural conscience. Such an understanding of Wesley would have facilitated an appropriate alternative for Methodist missionaries in starting dialogue with African people, yet such an understanding was apparently absent.

James Emman Kodwa Aggrey is quoted as saying: "Africans have always looked for someone like Christ Jesus."[8] Indeed, it was Christ who was the good news to the African people; the Christ who comes to us and meets the African people in their own cultural context to make them his disciples. If "culture shapes the human voice that answers the voice of Christ," then the Church in Africa needs to take the study of its cultural and religious traditional life seriously. Through the power of Christ, the Church in Africa should be given the opportunity to be the authentic Church of Christ on the continent, the Church that brings glory to Him who makes all things new (Rev. 21:9-26).

Summary

(1) The biblical and theological understanding of marriage has not yet been pursued within the African cultural context; rather, the practice in most churches is a copy of what was imported from overseas. Indeed, there is a need to reflect the importance and meaning of such events in people's life, both biblically and theologically, and yet that meaning should be related and expressed through concepts and practices people know and understand.

(2) The Christian faith does not deprive people of their cultural and social identity on their conversion to Christianity. Instead, the Christian gospel judges the culture and all social practices of a people, rejecting what is unacceptable, but affirming those cultural and social practices that mark one's identity. This is an ongoing

theological exercise that calls upon those who participate in such reflection to be fully cognizant of both the Christian faith and the culture involved.

(3) African people have always had some idea and conception of God. What missionaries brought to Africa was the knowledge of God through Christ. It is the Christ who was the new element knowledge of God through Christ, as God of love and forgiveness.

Chapter 7

Church Organizations

One of the characteristic features of the period 1921–1945 in the history of United Methodism in Southern Rhodesia was the formation of several organizations within the Church itself. While some of those organizations waned with the passing of time, others have continued to grow and have remained a vital part of the life of The United Methodist Church to this day. A close look at the origin of those organizations and the nature of their constitutions is indicative of how The United Methodist Church has come to understand itself, not only in Southern Rhodesia during that period but even more so in Zimbabwe today. We shall deal with four key organizations: *Vabvuwi veMethodist Episcopal Church* (Methodist Episcopal Church Men), *Rukwadzano rweVadzimai veMethodist Episcopal Church* (Women's Society of Christian Service), *The African Christian Convention*, and *Ngariende* (The African Missionary Society). In examining them, we have to ascertain whether they were influenced wholly from the outside or sprang out of the situation with which the Church was confronted in the country.

Vabvuwi veMethodist Episcopal Church (Methodist Episcopal Church Men)

The literal translation of the name of this organization should be Fishermen of the Methodist Episcopal Church for in Shona *vabvuwi* means fishermen. The organization started as a direct result of the revival of 1918 in The Methodist Episcopal Church in Southern Rhodesia.[1] The revival stands out as one of the occasions when Africans were able to respond to and to share the gospel in contextual ways. Just as the revival spread throughout the conference through individuals or groups going from one village to another, so some men organized themselves to continue that practice as a permanent way of doing evangelism. They communicated the gospel primarily through singing; in particular, singing hymns with African tunes and words that they formulated themselves. They traveled from one place to another and became known as *marombe* (homeless people).

Marombe in this particular case meant people who had left their homes, families, and everything else for something they considered special. In the case of these men, it was Christ whom they sought to follow. A problem arose when these men took the meaning of *marombe* too literally and abandoned their families and advocated asceticism, which for some took the form of abandoning rules of cleanliness. When the constitution of the organization came out, therefore, the first rule was to encourage members to adhere to cleanliness. The second rule was to remind the members of their family responsibilities. The name *marombe* was dropped and replaced by *vabvuwi* (fishermen). The meaning of the name *vabvuwi* was more appropriate for the task of the organization, that of bringing other people to Christ. Their purpose is stated in their constitution as "To bring others to Christ, to seek sinners and deepen their faith in God."[2]

Functionally, the Vabvuwi organization seems to be an arm of the *ecclesia*, going out to bring in new people. Yet, when it comes to the membership of the organization they are an *ecclesiola in ecclesia*, for they allow only those to join their membership who are already members of the Church. To this day, in order to be accepted into the Vabvuwi organization, one has to prove one's full membership of The United Methodist Church. All members must obey the rules, some of which are positive, such as the rule that a *mubvuwi* (a fisherman) should support his family. But there are several negative rules: a *mubvuwi* should not smoke, drink, play cards, enter dance halls, join in African dances, or other things that are considered to be the work of darkness. Every local church in The United Methodist Church in Zimbabwe is represented by this organization. In many of these local churches Vabvuwi groups have proved to be an effective arm of the church, particularly where the pastor has a good relationship with the group.

Rukwadzano rweVadzimai veMethodist Episcopal Church (Women's Society of Christian Service)

The origin of the Rukwadzano rweVadzimai veMethodist Episcopal Church is associated with Lydia Chimonyo, who started the organization in 1929 after the conference had approved such an organization in 1928. It started with theological students' wives at Old Mutare and some of the workers' wives who took some time for prayer each time they went out to look for firewood. Eventually, they organized themselves in a more formal way. They met every Sunday morning at about four o'clock in a church building at Mandisodza Village. Lydia Chimonyo, whose husband was then a theological student at Old Mutare, was the first official leader of the group in 1929.

During the Easter week of 1930, Old Mutare experienced another revival during which they had to close school for two days in order to give students and others enough time to share their evangelistic message. It is likely that the news of the women's organization at Old Mutare spread with the tide of the revival as preachers traveled to different villages. We have an impressive list of founding mothers along with Lydia Chimonyo, whose husbands were, for the most part, students at Old Mutare during that time. They are: Edith Marange, Lydia Mandizera, Lillian Machiri, Emily Rugayo, Emma Katsidzira, Judith Munjoma, Moud Chitombo, Elsi Sauramba, Cecilia Mawoyo, Lydia Chirewa, Martha Chikosi, Esther Mupikata, Naomi Makuto, Katherine Cheke, Lydia Kamusono, Esther Jangano, Helen Pedzeni, and Julia Chingono.

The fact that the majority of these women were wives of students training to become ministers in the Southern Rhodesia Annual Conference helps to explain the role of leadership that the ministers' wives have played in the organization ever since. The minister's wife came automatically to be the leader of the organization at every local church. At the conference level there have been ministers' wives who have kept the organization going. Even today, some women in The United Methodist Church in Zimbabwe still participate in the very early Sunday morning prayer meeting at their local churches. They have a biblical precedent for this practice in the women who were the first to get up on Easter Sunday to go to the tomb when Jesus appeared to Mary Magdalene after the resurrection (Mark 16:9). By their example they exhort the women to be first in the sanctuary every Sunday morning.

According to the constitution of the organization, the original purpose was "to promote the financial, social and spiritual interests of the Church."[3] The quotation is clearly taken from the Methodist *Discipline* and adopted for the Rhodesia situation. A statement of purpose of the organization revised in 1944 and 1960 reads a little differently:

> To show the abundant life of Jesus Christ to all women and older girls, to know Him and to do that which He desires; through the gospel, through healing and education, through meetings to better understand one another, and to work together with the Ngariende (Missionary) Society by helping the churches in the villages.[4]

The gospel mentioned above could, but should not, be perceived as separate from education and healing ministries, and the rest that follows. With this interpretation in mind, the corrected statement of purpose is more congenial to the spirit and practices of the organization as well as the spirit of Lydia Chimonyo than was the first one. This organization has lived up to its purpose. They have helped in meeting financial needs of the conference in many ways: providing funds for educational programs, scholarships, for medical work, for Conference Home Missions programs, pastors' salaries, and many other causes. Above all, they have been core prayer groups in the local churches.

Like Vabvuwi groups, Rukwadzano groups are *ecclesiola in ecclesia*. Here again, to be a member of the organization it is not enough to be a member of the Church. A woman has to prove herself. The members have uniform dresses and have regulations as to when these should be worn. For full members of the organization must follow this rule: "If a member of Rukwadzano does not live righteously she will be removed from membership and her uniform will be taken away." Probationers of the Church may not enter into full membership of the organization. This may suffice to illustrate why the Rukwadzano organization is considered to be the most rigidly organized group within The United Methodist Church in Zimbabwe to this day. Some of their rules are contrary to the way many young pastors want to see the Church move. Many young pastors raise the charge of legalism against the organization, when change seems to be the rhythm of life. This argument has caused a number of heated debates on the annual conference floor each time the Rukwadzano report is given.

Finally, it is appropriate to say a little more about Lydia Chimonyo, the first chairperson of the organization. She was born in 1892 at Sherukuru. Her father, Matura Duri, had two sons, Tambi and Gabriel, and one daughter, Makanatseyi, popularly known as

Nathaniel Jijita, *right*, one of the earliest Pastor Teachers.

Simeon Machiri, *left*, one of the earliest Pastor Teachers.

Thomas Marange,
right (1886–1972).
Ordained Deacon
1926, and Elder 1929.

David Mandisodza,
left (1887–1963).
The first African
to be ordained in
the Methodist
Episcopal Church
of Rhodesia in
1921, and Elder,
1929.

Clifford Faku, *left* (1882–1946) was ordained Deacon after 1921 and Elder 1929.

Benjamin Katsidzira, *right*, was ordained Deacon in 1926, Elder in 1930.

Eddy Greeley, *left*,
came to Southern
Rhodesia in 1900
and started Boys
School at Old
Mutare in 1901.

Jason Chikosi, *right*,
one of the earliest
Pastor Teachers.

Dr. Kurewa's mother, about 96 years old, with his sister, Mrs. Catherine Radzokota.

John W. Z. Kurewa, just after receiving a courtesy ordination as Deacon by Bishop Richard Renines, Bloomington, Indiana, 1962.

John Kurewa, Secretary to the Parliament of Zimbabwe, at a Parliamentary Conference.

John and Gertrude Kurewa.

Lydia after her baptism. When Sherukuru Methodist Episcopal Church came into existence in 1907, Lydia's brother Gabriel (after baptism) quickly took a leadership position as a church steward.

In accordance with one of the Shona customs, then Lydia's spouse had already been chosen for her by her parents. She was supposed to be married to an already married man in the Muchena area, just about ten kilometers northeast of Old Mutare Mission. Lydia was taken to the village of her husband-to-be in 1914; she managed to escape from the village and walked to Old Mutare Mission where she took refuge. She started school immediately; and in 1915, Lydia was married to Obediah Chimonyo, a widowed seminary student.

According to a testimony given one Sunday afternoon in 1945 at the Sherukuru Church by Lydia's brother Tambi, Lydia had associated with the Sherukuru congregation right from its origin in 1907. The author was old enough to be present and to witness Tambi's testimony of conversion in the 1950s. Tambi had a dream on a Saturday evening. According to the dream, Tambi had dreamt of vomiting excessively. In the dream, when someone asked him to eat what he had vomited, Tambi refused to do so. On waking from his dream the following Sunday morning he went to see my father, Isaac Kurewa, who was the head steward of the congregation, then at Sherukuru in order to seek interpretation of the dream. It happened that Tambi was a well-known person at Sherukuru. He was not a member of any church. Instead, Tambi was a *n'anga* (diviner, herbalist, or medicine man). Living not only a typical African traditional life, in the Church's eyes Tambi lived a life which seemed a contradiction to the life of faith in Christ in that he had three wives and often brewed traditional beer.

Seeing the opportunity to communicate the gospel, the saving power of God for the salvation of anyone who believes (Rom. 1:16), my father interpreted Tambi's dream of vomiting as a decisive act on Tambi's part—a confession of his sinful life that needed no repetition. No wonder that in his dream Tambi would not eat what he had vomited. Tambi got the message. That Sunday afternoon, Tambi attended the worship service and gave his testimony.

In his testimony, Tambi shocked listeners by announcing publicly his commitment to a new life in Jesus Christ. He publicly confessed a grudge he had held against the Sherukuru United Methodist Church for a long time because the church's pastor-teacher, Philip Perayi (1907–1909) had advised and urged his sister, Lydia, to consider taking refuge at Old Mutare Mission to avoid the pre-arranged marriage with which she did not agree. Following that statement, he thanked his sister for seeing the light that then dawned for him. He asked for forgiveness from the congregation for his hostility to the Sherukuru Church. Tambi went on to ask the church for two things, neither of which was fulfilled. One was that he be baptized, and the other was for a prayer meeting at his home. He proclaimed that since he was an old man he would leave the decision about his three wives to them, for they were old enough to decide for themselves.

The pastor-teacher Eric Murahwa sent a word to the pastor of the circuit, who happened to be Tambi's brother-in-law, Obediah Chimonyo, together with his wife, Lydia, who received the news with gladness. The pastor arranged to have Tambi baptized the following Sunday; and the Sherukuru congregation accepted Tambi's invitation to hold a prayer meeting with the whole family that following Saturday. Tambi's death preceded the two events; he died in his sleep the following Thursday night.

So Lydia came from a family that was sensitive to God's activities in the life of people. After her marriage to Obediah Chimonyo, Lydia was known by her vigorous discipline in matters of spiritual formation and development. To this day, there are two places at Old Mutare that are associated with her because she frequently went to those places to pray.

A claim is made that Lydia received a baptism of the Holy Spirit at Manyarara Methodist Episcopal Church, a congregation that no longer exists because of the Land Apportionment Act. The site of the church was about six kilometers north of Old Mutare Mission. Apparently, Lydia had gone there to cultivate *tsenza* (a tropical, tuberous plant); and then decided to attend an afternoon worship service when she experienced the baptism. Subsequently, Lydia became known as a very effective local preacher, Sunday school teacher, and the first chairperson of the Rukwadzano rweVadzimai in the then Southern Rhodesia Annual Conference of the Methodist Church.

Her last meeting with the Women's Organization was held in the Marange area in September 1940. On the last day of that meeting Lydia is said to have preached and then to have started singing ceaselessly, to the point that she seemed to be going out of her mind. According to an eye witness, she then bowed and picked up soil in her hands and threw it to the people—especially to where missionaries and pastors were sitting. She announced to all as she threw the soil that she had preached the gospel as she had been called by her Master; she exhorted preachers to preach the word, and to pray all the time. Again, she announced to all that her time on earth was limited. After returning to Chitenderano where her husband was the pastor, Lydia passed away on 25 October 1940 and was buried there.

On Friday, 6 September 1991, the Rukwadzano rweVadzimai of the United Methodist Church of the Zimbabwe Annual Conference held a special memorial service at the place where Lydia was buried. The emphasis of the worship service was to memorialize Lydia's leadership, which was characterized by native originality, dynamism, and a vision for the Rukwadzano rweVadzimai as an organization that was to bring renewal in the life of the whole Church. In memory of Lydia, the Rukwadzano rweVadzimai put a tombstone on her grave and Bishop Abel T. Muzorewa delivered the message of the day and led the memorial worship service. She was held in such great esteem that the Zimbabwe Annual Conference still talks about her dedication to the Christian life and her dynamic leadership not only to the women's organization, but to the whole annual conference.

The African Christian Convention

In 1928 the Rhodesia Mission Conference approved a recommendation to start the African Christian Convention, an annual meeting for the African Christians in the then Methodist Episcopal Church. The idea was to start something that would give African ministers and laymen the opportunity to discuss some of the problems the Church was facing without their discussions being dominated by missionaries, as was the case at the annual conference. According to the constitution of the organization, its orientation was broad. The organization could talk about everything that they found to be a problem and send their recommendations to the annual conference. The reports of the Christian Convention to the conference show that many issues were discussed, including methods for improving African homes and sanitation, solving educational problems in the villages, urging church members to adopt the practice of saving money at the post office or at the bank, and helping people understand Christian marriage.

The greatest contribution of the African Christian Convention Organization in the life of The Methodist Episcopal Church from the 1930s through the 1950s was to serve as a custodian to the African leaders, until such a time when Africans were able to stand on their own feet. African leaders needed the opportunity to discuss their problems and their own hopes and ideas of their own church in a context where they were able to express themselves. As their voices began to draw some attention by the middle of the 1950s, and even to dominate by the end of the 1960s, the African Christian Convention began dying a natural death. The last meeting of the Christian Convention was held in 1969; a vote was passed not to print any report of it in the Conference Journal.

Ngariende (The African Missionary Society)

As early as 1927 the Board of Home Missions and Church Extension organization was started in the life of the then Methodist Episcopal Church in Southern Rhodesia. Of the twelve members elected from the conference floor, six were missionaries and six were African. It does not seem that much was done by that organization except to raise some benevolence monies. Therefore, in 1938 a reorganization of the board took place which resulted in a new organization called The African Missionary Society of The Methodist Episcopal Church in Rhodesia. The aim of the organization was "to spread the Gospel of our Lord Jesus Christ." Josiah Chimbadzwa, who was an able preacher, was the first chairperson of this new organization.

The organization which started as a church board thus became a predominantly African organization. Did missionaries feel that they had brought the gospel to the Africans but it was now time for the Africans to take the gospel to their own fellows? Or was it the African people who felt that after the missionaries had brought the gospel to them, it was now their turn to move on to areas of their land where many had not heard the gospel? Or was it both? At any rate, the meaning of ngariende is literally, "let it go," "it" meaning the gospel. The title of the organization might more appropriately be Ngariende Vangeri, meaning "let the gospel go." The idea was not to preserve the gospel for oneself but to let it move on to others.

Whichever way the idea came, Ngariende became a challenge to African Methodists. They had to organize themselves to move on to those who had not heard the good news of Christ Jesus.

In May 1939 three men volunteered on behalf of the African Missionary Society to go to Mount Darwin in Chief Dotito's area to study the needs of the people there and to ascertain the possibility of establishing a mission from which the preaching of the gospel could be launched in the area. The Native Commissioner of Mount Darwin and Chief Dotito himself had shown signs of interest in this missionary enterprise by the African Missionary Society of The Methodist Episcopal Church. Yet for reasons not mentioned, the plans were aborted. Having failed to gain entrance into Chief Dotito's area, another team of three men was sent to Chief Chikwizo's area in December 1941. Chief Chikwizo favored the idea of starting missionary work in his area and at the request of the African Missionary Society, Bishop Springer appointed Ebson Zimonte, who was ordained, and his wife, Lydia, as the first African missionaries sent by the annual conference to Chikwizo early in 1942. While he organized church work, his wife, a trained teacher, organized school work.

In the last thirty years every local United Methodist congregation has at least heard about the Chikwizo missionary projects and many of these churches have supported these projects. The problem with the Ngariende as a whole, however, was that nothing had been done beyond the work at Chikwizo. Neither did the work in the Chikwizo area move as fast as the supporting churches were expecting. Five congregations had been in the area, along with two schools and a clinic, and until 1966 these were still dependent on the support from Ngariende. To many people the Chikwizo work appeared as a spoiled child. When I was appointed to serve as pastor in the area in 1960, I could not help but see a pattern: the dependence of Chikwizo on the conference paralleled that of the Zimbabwe Annual Conference on churches in the United States.

Later on, Ngariende and the Committee on Evangelism merged, forming what became known as the Conference Board of Ngariende. With an appointed executive secretary of that new board in the 1970s, The United Methodist Church was able to reach out into new areas like Rwenya, Chesa, Mkota, Shapuri, and others, but not necessarily in the style that was used at Chikwizo.

The United Methodist Church in Zimbabwe, as part of the

African Central Conference through the guidance of the Board of Ngariende, was also able to participate in the Botswana missionary and ecumenical project initiated in 1968 by action of the Africa Central Conference.

Because mission is the very heart of a living Church, the Church can never afford time for rest. Dr. David Bosch is correct in saying that true mission causes unrest in the Church.[5] This seems to be exactly what has been happening in the life of The United Methodist Church in Zimbabwe through the Board of Ngariende. The United Methodist Church has been searching for the right strategy to reach out to those in need of the ministry of Christ Jesus. One of the easiest things to do for churches that have had missionary leadership for a long time is to fall into a model of imitation. This might have been the case with Chikwizo, where after those many years things did not seem to move. Maybe the Church in Southern Rhodesia was trying to imitate the Church in America. The latter had the money and a very sophisticated organization which the former could not afford. While it is important for the Church anywhere to know how other branches operate, the Church in Zimbabwe needs to continue struggling and striving for strategies that will work in her own situation. Peculiar situations call for unique and relevant ministries. This is where sensitivity and obedience to God's call and guidance come in.

Summary

(1) Both the Vabvuwi and Rukwadzano organizations understood themselves as organizations within The Methodist Episcopal Church. They had their own rules and regulations, in addition to those for membership in The Methodist Episcopal Church. There is a certain fear on the part of others of the strong tendency in these organizations to be legalistic in their understanding of the Christian faith. However, functionally they are at the same time an evangelistic arm of the Church.

(2) We have pointed out that the greatest contribution of the African Christian Convention in the 1930s through the 1950s was its role as the training ground for African leadership.

(3) Finally, the name of the Ngariende organization should be Ngariende Vangeri, meaning "let the gospel go"; that is, let the gospel be shared with those beyond our frontiers. While mission is

the very heart of the Church, the Church in Africa should not imitate the West in accomplishing its mission. Paul Lin, a Chinese scholar, speaking at a Third World seminar in relation to economic problems said, "No one can pioneer with a model; every people has its own way."[6] It is important for the Church in Africa to recognize that every people has its own models, especially in evangelization. For example, the term *ngariende* evokes not only historical and theological significance, it also triggers a perception of a contextual model of doing evangelism which is manageable for United Methodists in Zimbabwe. The Board of Ngariende, for awhile, was able to send lay preachers into new areas to investigate possibilities of opening up preaching places as well as detecting needs of people. These men could be either local preachers or a team of the Vabvuwi veUnited Methodist Church. During their investigative visits, contact is made with local chiefs and preaching meetings held in villages. By the time an official report is presented to the church hierarchy, the Vabvuwi will have started the process of evangelization. This is what we mean by saying Vabvuwi are an evangelistic arm of the Church; also this is an example of the Church exploring indigenous models of fulfilling God's mission in their cultural context. Unless the Church in Africa recognizes that they are a people with their own cultural models of evangelization, they will always remain imitators. With rapid church growth on the continent today, the African Church has much to teach peoples of other continents about Christianity in Africa.

Part III

The Church in Mission
(1945–1997)

In 1939 The Methodist Episcopal Church became The Methodist Church. During this period its name was changed to The United Methodist Church (1968). A new theological consciousness arose, not just in The United Methodist Church but also in the life of other denominations.

The 1960s mark an era of ecumenism throughout Africa. In that spirit of ecumenism there seemed to be a very conscious and sincere effort on the part of the churches to pull down denominational walls, not only for cooperation but also for purposes of organic union. The challenge of God's mission and the willingness of churches to engage in ecumenical projects seemed to have brought about the realization of the importance of the unity of the Church of Christ.

In the following five chapters, there is a sense in which The United Methodist Church is submerged, because it is the whole Church in Zimbabwe or Africa that is of greater importance. A new concept of the Church had dawned on the continent of Africa.

Chapter 8

The Church and African Nationalism

Early 1945 marked the publication of a book by Bishop Newell Booth, a missionary who had just been elected to the episcopacy of Africa the previous year. The book, entitled *The Cross Over Africa*, contained a very appropriate catchphrase in referring to the African situation then, describing the African as "a stranger in his own land."[1] Many people who had not even read the book began to use that phrase. It was a phrase packed with truth regarding the way the African had been treated under colonial rule.

Following the end of World War II, Southern Rhodesia like other African countries was confronted by a new consciousness of nationalism. Slogans such as "Freedom now," "Nyika yedu" (our country), and "Majority rule now" became common expressions in the country, especially in the late 1950s. In this chapter we will discuss first, the roots of African nationalism in Southern Rhodesia, and second, the African Church and African nationalism.

Roots of African Nationalism in Southern Rhodesia

Nationalism does not happen in a vacuum. Certain political, social, economic, and religious conditions have to be present. Someone has correctly said that African nationalism displayed one feature very clearly: namely, that it is the notion of history as a past to be preserved or a task to be undertaken. If it is true that it is always in the past that one finds identity and meaning to life, then the worst thing that can happen to a person is to be deprived of his or her history and heritage. For Zimbabweans, that past had always been linked with the ancient Zimbabwe. African nationalism in Southern Rhodesia was prompted by a number of factors, including the ancient Zimbabwe empire, the Matabele and Mashona Wars against colonial settlers, and post-World War II nationalism.

107

First, let us look at the ancient Zimbabwe empire. The teaching of history in colonial schools always began with colonization. The pre-colonization period was safely neglected, and, instead, time was spent studying the history of the British Empire, which, in fact, undermined the identity of the African people. In Zimbabwe there is the famous Great Zimbabwe, about twenty-seven kilometers from Masvingo. Zimbabwe literally means a big house of stones. During the colonial years, the origin of the Great Zimbabwe was ascribed to all kinds of foreign people, never to the people of Zimbabwe. Today it is common knowledge that the Great Zimbabwe was the work of the Shona people. More significantly, Zimbabwe also stands for a great empire and culture that once existed. In order to understand post-World War II Rhodesian nationalism during this period, we need to take a brief look at the history of Zimbabwe before colonization by the British.

According to one distinguished Zimbabwean historian, Stanlake Samkange, by the end of the fourth century the first group of the Bantu migration from the north southward had arrived in what is now Zimbabwe. These people and even their successors, still built with stone although the use of iron and the working with iron techniques had already been introduced.

Among the later immigrants who reached Zimbabwe in about the tenth century were ancestors of the Shona people.[2] The Shona dominated all other groups that had settled in the area. Early in the fifteenth century a dynasty arose among the Shona, later to be identified as the Rozvi.[3] This dynasty is said to have had so brilliant a military career that they won for themselves a name of praise— Mwene Mutapa (meaning "master pillager")—a title which was changed by the Portuguese to Munumutapa. A later member of this dynasty, Munumutapa Mutota, was faced with a shortage of salt in the area. The desire to control all the salt deposits led Munumutapa Mutota to launch another military campaign. In the process he welded several strong states and lesser ones into a great empire,[4] which extended from the Zambezi River, passing south beyond the Limpopo River into the present province of Transvaal, and from the Indian Ocean to the Kalahari Desert. What is at present Mozambique, Zimbabwe, Transvaal, and Botswana constituted Munumutapa's empire. Within that empire there existed some twenty-five kingdoms that were ruled by vassal princes who acknowledged the emperor of Munumutapa as their great Lord and paid him tributes of gold. Munumutapa's royal residence, which is known today as the Great Zimbabwe, probably reached the height of its fame in the middle of the sixteenth century.[5]

After his brilliant conquests Munumutapa Mutota moved his capital from Great Zimbabwe to the northern part of the country, that is, to Dande. When the Great Munumutapa Mutota died, his son Matope became the next emperor. Like his father, Matope was a brilliant military man. He extended the borders of the empire even further. The problem came with Nyahuma, who took over after Matope. He was not of the same military calibre as his predecessors and this gave the dissatisfied chiefs in the southern part of the empire the opportunity to set up one of their own men as ruler in the south. He became known as Changamire (a title which means king). Immediately Changamire rebelled against Nyahuma and killed him in battle. Changamire became the emperor but later was killed by the son of Nyahuma.[6] As a consequence of this back-and-forth struggle, the empire remained under two dynasties, the Munumutapa in the north and the Changamire, who covered more territory and were stronger, in the south.

For a long time the Portuguese had waited to find a way to obtain the gold that had made Munumutapa the famous and rich emperor he was. By the year 1610, the Portuguese were close enough to take advantage of the split in the empire. They made Munumutapa surrender all rights and titles to his mines. From then on, the Munumutapa dynasty became a puppet of the Portuguese and was never to rise again. Also, the Changamire's rule was finally terminated by Mzilikazi, king of the Mandebele people, about 1840. That marked the end of the ancient Zimbabwe empire.

This brief look at the pre-colonial history of Zimbabwe has been necessary for two reasons: (1) To perceive Africans as a people who were fragmented and who were only brought together by colonial domination is a fallacy. Ironically, it is the other way round, for out of Munumutapa's empire colonists formed no less than five countries or colonies. (2) Even more important, the African people in Zimbabwe have a history that precedes the colonial period. That history is beginning to reveal the rich culture that African people had, of which colonial governments deliberately attempted to deprive them. A good example is the Great Zimbabwe. No wonder most African political parties' names in Zimbabwe always included the name "Zimbabwe." They realized that they have a past to identify with, a past from which nationalists had to project their political programs.

The second factor is the Matabele and Mashona Wars against colonial settlers, but before turning to the wars we need to look briefly at the African history surrounding colonialism. Mzilikazi, king of the Matabele people southwest of Zimbabwe had brought Changamire's empire to an end. He was succeeded to the throne by his son, Lobengula. On 30 October 1888, Lobengula signed the Rudd Concession as king of Matebeleland, and allegedly of Mashonaland as well, granting mining rights in his area to Cecil Rhodes to the exclusion of any other white groups.[7] He took this action after hesitating a long time, constantly under threat of attack unless he did so.[8] When he realized what he had done by signing the papers, Lobengula sent envoys to the queen in England but it was too late. By 12 September 1890, the Pioneer Column from the south had reached Harare. On the following day the British flag was ceremonially hoisted as a sign of occupation of the land.

Lobengula could not change the train of events after he had put his "X" mark on the Rudd Concession papers, although he tried. More whites came into the land, not passing on to Mashonaland as Lobengula would have preferred, but staying in Matabeleland. The only way to change things was to fight. He must have welcomed the opportunity when it came. Some of the Shona people around Masvingo area cut the telegraph line from Cape Town. This was brought to Lobengula's attention, and in order to punish the Shona people Lobengula invaded the area, but the people sought refuge in the white settlement. Lobengula demanded that these people be released to him but he was denied permission to punish them. That gave him the opportunity to strike at the white settlers. Lobengula was defeated. His capital, which stood where Bulawayo stands today, was burned. Lobengula fled to the north. A patrol under Major Allan Wilson pursued Lobengula northward. One of Lobengula's men, Mhlahlo, reported what happened:

> We then saw a number of white men riding along. There were about thirty. We surrounded them and started to fight. They got off their horses and fired at us over them. All the horses were killed, and then the white men, those that were left, all of whom were wounded, lay on their backs and held their rifles between their feet and fired. After a little while the firing stopped, and we knew the cartridges were finished. We then rushed up and assegaied

the remainder who covered their eyes with their hands [an assegai is a short-handled, long-bladed stabbing spear]. We lost many more than the number of whites killed, for they were men indeed and fought us for many hours. We never fought again after this fight and soon after we had peace. . . .[9]

They never found Lobengula, who apparently perished in his flight.

Even with Lobengula out of the way there was still tension throughout the land. Africans resented being pushed around as the settlers tried to administrate them. The result was rebellion both in Matebeleland (1894) and in Mashonaland (1896). In both areas, rebellion by Africans began with a massacre of isolated families, particularly in mining areas. The reasons given for the Africans' rebellion were taxation, forced labor services, brutality of the police, and resentment that thousands of Lobengula's cattle had been taken by the white people. It was indeed a range of grievances.

Since our task is not to write the history of Zimbabwe as such, but an attempt to locate the roots of African nationalism, we return to two issues: (1) African nationalists in the 1950s and 1960s challenged the Rudd Concession, not only on the ground that Lobengula was threatened when he signed it, but also that he did not understand the deal or the implications. His sending of envoys to the queen is a good argument in the case. One author, Gann, believes that the Matebele people understood what they were signing because Reverend Charles Helm, a member of the London Missionary Society, explained everything to them. Unfortunately, the argument is not very convincing; instead, it puts the missionaries in an awkward position, for Reverend Charles Helm even signed his name on the Rudd Concession as a witness. (2) The Matabele War and the ensuing rebellion, both in Matebeleland and Mashonaland, always stood as a symbol of the African struggle to claim the land of their birth. Therefore, African nationalists in the 1950s and 1960s appealed to the memory of those struggles.

The last factor is post-World War II nationalism. World War II is acknowledged as a major factor in the awakening of the African consciousness. Fighting side by side with white soldiers taught the Africans that they were all human. As Ndabaningi Sithole said, for the African to see the so-called civilized people butcher one another as the so-called savages of Africa were accused of doing was quite an experience. It became clear that the white man was just as savage as anyone else—an eye-opening realization.

African nationalism has rightly been recognized as being first, continental; and second, territorial. This important factor is part of the reason for the Pan-African meetings, beginning in 1945 at Manchester, England, with Africans who were eventually to become the political leaders in Africa. When Africans think of leaders in terms of the whole continent, Kwame Nkrumah will always remain an inspiration. It was he who said at one of the meetings:

> I have never regarded the struggle for independence of Gold Coast as an isolated incident but always as a part of general world historical pattern. The African in every territory of this vast continent has been awakened and the struggle for freedom will go on.[10]

In Southern Rhodesia the first nationalist party, the African National Congress of Southern Rhodesia (ANC), was organized in 1957 with Joshua Nkomo as president. The ANC was very successful in mobilizing discontent against discriminatory laws and policies of the white government in the country, and also in bringing about a new political consciousness among the African people. It was time for an awakening. The organization created and provided African people with a platform from which their political, social, and economic grievances were publicly vocalized. The impact was so great that the ANC was viewed by whites as an ultimate threat to their security. Therefore it was not surprising that on 26 February 1959 the African National Congress of Southern Rhodesia was banned and its leaders were arrested.

Again, our immediate interest is not the history of African political consciousness, as important as it is. Rather, we are trying to provide a framework for the situation in which the Church found itself struggling to understand its mission in the 1950s and 1960s. It is therefore important to mention that after the banning of the ANC other political organizations emerged, different in name but with the same goals. Among them were the Zimbabwe African People's Union (ZAPU) which was formed in December 1961 with Joshua Nkomo as president, and the Zimbabwe African National Union (ZANU) which was formed in August 1963 with Ndabaningi Sithole as president, followed later by Robert Mugabe. These political parties were also eventually banned from the country. This was the situation when the Pearce Commission arrived in January 1972 to investigate the Douglas Home Proposals for settlement as an attempt to terminate Rhodesia's rebellion. That occasion witnessed the emergence of another group which eventually became a political party in the country, the United African National Council (UANC) with Bishop Abel T. Muzorewa of The United Methodist Church as president. Later, in the mid-1970s, after Robert Mugabe became president of ZANU, a raproachment between ZANU and ZAPU resulted in the formation of the Patriotic Front (PF), which received major support from Rhodesia's majority-ruled neighbors. At the end of the decade, Mugabe led ZANU to victory in the election that resulted in independence; he became the first prime minister of Zimbabwe in 1980. Nkomo and ZAPU broke with Mugabe's government in the early 1980s, but a new agreement between the two leaders led to a merger of their parties to form the ZANU (PF), and in 1987 Mugabe became Zimbabwe's first executive president, with Nkomo its vice-president

The Church and Nationalism in Africa

How did the Church understand African nationalism? Most people in Africa would have no problem understanding what we are talking about, for everyone has experienced nationalism in one way or another and could very easily identify the manifestation of its spirit. As Robert Rotberg said, in spite of all the obvious manifestations of nationalism, "its spirit remains, like most spirits, capable only of inexact description. It is, in essence, pretty much what it is."

This is indeed, the way in which the Church in Africa came to understand the spirit of African nationalism; it came to grips with it only as it manifested itself. Thus Alan Paton, a great Christian spokesman of South Africa, in his paper to the All-Africa Conference of Churches at Ibadan in 1958, made the point that African nationalism was inevitable in all its manifestations. At its best, he saw it as self-respect and integrity in a person; but, at its worst, he perceived it as arrogance, selfishness, and even cruelty in a person. Dr. K. A. Busia of Ghana interpreted African nationalism primarily as a demand for racial equality—Africans demanding acceptance as equals in the human family. Ndabaningi Sithole of Zimbabwe saw many new elements in African nationalism: a new African awareness, a new self-evaluation, a new sense of destiny, a new approach to problems facing the African, a new way of removing

113

other-determination and of establishing self-determination. This was indicative of efforts by the African leaders from all walks of life to face the issue of African nationalism. And the Church in Africa as a whole, as well as in Zimbabwe in particular, took African nationalism seriously.

Next, we shall examine the relationship of the Church with nationalism in Africa by looking at the Church's definition of nationalism, the Bible as a "subversive" book, education for indigenous leadership, and the involvement of The United Methodist Church.

The Church's Definition of Nationalism

In 1963 at Kampala the All-Africa Conference of Churches made a significant statement about African nationalism, and defined it as "the common desire of a people to work together for their emancipation from any form of bondage, whether colonial, economic, social or racial."[11]

Four forms of nationalism were distinguished: nationalism working towards freedom and independence; nationalism working towards the creation of national cohesion (particularly important for newly independent nations); nationalism of older nations which, even when repudiated, manifested itself through the attempt to conserve the traditional way of life; and, nationalism which evolved into an ideology of totalitarian character, e.g. National Socialism.

Two factors were brought up in the attempt to understand nationalism. (1) History is both a past to be preserved and a task to be undertaken. Theologically it was emphasized that history was always the object of God's rule where humans' obedience as expected. (2) Authority is the goal of emancipation for the responsibility of nationhood. The authority envisaged is exercised by God over people and nations and entrusted to people within nations. The Assembly perceived that God at times can use historical movements such as nationalism as an instrument of God's divine rule.

It became necessary to define the limits within which nationalism might be a form of Christian obedience and beyond which it could become demonic. Thus the following statement was made:

Nationalism must aim at the establishment of freedom and justice and respect of human dignity, instead of being concerned for

114

power for its sake. It must work for the unity and cohesion of the nation instead of serving the power of one group at the expense of others. This does not mean the exclusion of a strong authority, but it does mean that strong authority must not work for the exclusive benefit of one group of the community. Nationalism should be open to, and concerned for the establishment of international solidarity instead of expressing the will to dominate other nations.[12]

This statement of the Kampala All-Africa Conference of Churches is based upon the experiences of African churches not only with nationalism, but also with the Christian faith. In other words, the Church in Africa did not seek to isolate itself from the social, political, economic, and cultural issues that its nations were facing. For this was where God might need them in the ministry of reconciliation.

The Bible as a "Subversive" Book

Guy Clutton Brock related the story of forty policemen visiting the Cold Comfort Farm Society, on 18 November 1970, at 5:30 A.M. He describes how the police gathered plastic bags, papers, letters, and books with a political tinge to them. Then he goes on to say: "Neither dope nor pornography were found, nor letters from Peking or Moscow. Our Bibles were left to continue subverting us."[13]

The message of the Bible has always proved powerful and influential. The message of God, who loved the world to such an extent that He gave His own Son (John 3:16), so that all who are baptized in Christ Jesus can no longer be looked upon as either Jew or Greek (Gal. 3:2), has always proved to be an earthshaking message, especially in colonially ruled Africa. How could one possibly proclaim such a message without going against the then government's doctrine, for example, of apartheid which upheld divisive measures for different races, seeking to serve the political, economic, and social needs of one group at the expense of all others?

No matter how many books the colonial regimes banned from entering their countries, as did Southern Rhodesia in the 1950s and 1960s, the Bible proved subversive each time its pages were opened. The Bible speaks to the African experiences of life in many ways. For example, in the Old Testament there is Moses leading the children of Israel from Egyptian bondage. Although it took Israel forty years to get to the "promised land," still they arrived according to God's promise. There are stories of Ahab and Naboth. The former usurped the latter's vineyard against the law of Israel (Num. 36:7). But Naboth's courage was not all in vain (1 Kings 21:1-22). In the New Testament there is the central theme of God as loving Father, who through His Son has created a fellowship which knows no color. Constantly, the worth and dignity of man in the sight of God is emphasized (Matt. 10:29). All these elements of the Christian faith are the fertile ground on which African nationalism thrived. During the 1950s and 1960s The United Methodist Church stood with all other Christians in Southern Rhodesia who struggled to relate the biblical message to the situation in Southern Africa.

Educating for Indigenous Leadership

It has been pointed out by Africans themselves that in Africa there is a close link between education and African nationalism. It is education that has provided the African with new ideas about natural rights, human dignity, liberty, equality of men and women, and so on. Busia quotes the English philosopher G. Lows Dickensen as saying, "Whatever men may say or think, ideas are the greatest force in the world." Some preacher has said, "There is nothing more powerful than an idea for which the time has come." If the forcefulness of ideas is true and new ideas are acquired through education, then the African has been on the right path in his pursuit of education. The question arises to what extent the churches in Africa have helped with education in the crisis of nationalism. To be specific, what role did The United Methodist Church play in Southern Rhodesia?

The United Methodist Church in Zimbabwe always sympathized with the cause and efforts of African nationalism. It believed that a nationalism which aimed at establishing freedom, justice, and respect for human dignity for all citizens of the country, was in keeping with the spirit of the Christian faith. It endeavored to see that God's mission was accomplished by involvement in such a way that nationalism became a blessing and not a curse to the nation. Consequently, The United Methodist Church in Zimbabwe accepted a challenge that nationalism presented in the 1950s and 1960s. It moved beyond education for the Church to education for the nation and world.

From the beginning the Church has been involved in education. But most churches had educated the African for the immediate needs of the church as an institution and denominational programs such as the ordained ministry, teachers for church schools, and nurses. This was an education obtainable within the country and in many churches meant nothing more than high school education. Many missionaries did not see the need for the African minister to have college or university training; for what mattered more to them than higher education was the power of the Holy Spirit.

In The United Methodist Church the dramatic change came with the vision of one man. In his book *The Unpopular Missionary*, Bishop Ralph Dodge tells of a conversation he had with an African pastor of another denomination. The Bishop asked him why his church had produced such outstanding leaders. The reply from the African pastor was, "We had a missionary who inspired us." In a way, these words described Bishop Dodge, too. He was a man of vision, not only in matters of the Church, but also for the country as a whole. He saw the need for indigenous leadership both in the Church and for the nation. He was always free to talk with both African church leaders and nationalists. When he saw needs, he took action. Thus, in 1961 Bishop Dodge inaugurated a program of scholarships to enable African students to study overseas. Before then, the Southern Rhodesia Annual Conference had never had more than five students overseas at one time. In 1961, fifty-seven students were abroad. Married students were accompanied by their wives, who were either enrolled as full-time students or were taking some courses. By 1962 the number had risen to over seventy students. This was not without opposition, primarily from some missionaries. But Bishop Dodge's investment paid a dividend. One only needs to look at Zimbabwe today to see the leadership exerted by the beneficiaries of those scholarships, both in the Church and in other positions, and to appreciate Bishop Dodge's courageous strategy.

Behind the actions of Bishop Dodge there was a vision which he freely shared with African pastors and laymen alike, a way of looking at life as a whole. The concept of the wholeness of life is very African and even more it is deeply rooted in the New Testament. Unfortunately, the gospel had been preached by some in Africa espousing the Platonic idea of the soul and the body being diametrically opposed to and separated from each other. The body

117

could be neglected; all that was necessary was to preach the salvation of the soul. But in his episcopal leadership Bishop Dodge labored to show that the gospel touched the whole person, and this concept in itself was inevitably revolutionary. The gospel touched the spiritual, political, social, economic, and cultural aspects of human life. The Church was not only an agitator of change, according to Bishop Dodge, but even more, the originator of a revolution. Bishop Dodge described this revolution of the Church as nonviolent. "But is no less a revolution," he said.

Such a view allowed Bishop Dodge to help The United Methodist Church in Southern Rhodesia to look at African nationalism positively and also with a sense of responsibility. The Church had to help educate young men and women for leadership beyond the Church in other areas of life. This he described as the task of building bridges of understanding between races and tribes wherever conflict was likely to occur.

The Involvement of The United Methodist Church

In responding to the challenges of the late 1950s and the 1960s The United Methodist Church relied heavily on leadership from the Social Concerns Committee. With the Unilateral Declaration of Independence (UDI) by the white Rhodesian government in November 1965, accompanied by various measures for perpetuating the white rule in Southern Rhodesia, it was not easy for any organization or church to operate in the country.

The United Methodist Church, as we now know it, had accepted the cause of African nationalism as an inevitable phenomenon of the time and had sought ways to be involved constructively. Under the leadership of the Christian Social Concerns Committee the conference wrestled in 1962 with the issue of preparing young African people for a political career. The first step was for the conference to approve making their Church buildings available for constructive political meetings. The work was so successful that in 1963 the conference urged all district superintendents and pastors to see to it that every local church had a local committee of the Christian Social Concerns. Then more and more students returned from abroad to join the ranks. Throughout the 1950s and 1960s, The United Methodist Church was strongly identified with the spirit of African nationalism. It spoke strongly against the government on several issues: the banning of African nationalist parties; security legislation, particularly under the guise of "law and order"; the Land Tenure Act of 1969, which required churches to register as voluntary associations; and the 5 percent cut in government grants for teachers' salaries. These were all controversial national issues in which the Church was deeply involved.

Nationalism did not remain outside the church walls. The United Methodist Church in Zimbabwe had to face the spirit of nationalism within its own institution. It did so by encouraging interchangeable housing for missionaries and African staff at all mission centers. In a 1961 newsletter, Bishop Dodge advised missionaries to work themselves out of their jobs by seeing to it that an African was trained for replacement. The writer recalls a lady missionary reacting emotionally in a meeting at Old Mutare Mission, "What are we all going to do if Africans take our jobs?" The change of orientation was not easy for a number of missionaries, but through openness and even confrontation of missionaries and African leaders in some of the consultations, feelings of hostility and mistrust began to dissolve. Gradually the idea of "A New Church in a New Africa" began to gain more ground.

Summary

(1) African nationalism in the then Southern Rhodesia has been deeply involved in the new awareness of the historical heritage of the ancient Empire of Zimbabwe, with Munumutapa as one supreme ruler.

(2) African nationalism in Southern Rhodesia could certainly be located in one geographical area. But the spirit in African nationalism is more continental than just territorial.

(3) There was a sound definition of nationalism as "the common desire of a people to work together for their emancipation from any form of bondage, whether colonial, economic, social or racial." In Southern Rhodesia, throughout the 1950s, 1960s, and 1970s, the task of nationalism was to work toward freedom and independence.

(4) The United Methodist Church with several other churches in the country believed that historical movements such as nationalism, could very easily be God's instrument to establish freedom, justice, and human dignity for all. Therefore, the Methodists were not ashamed to be involved. It was this kind of thinking that

enabled several church leaders in the country to be involved in the struggle for political freedom and independence of their own people. While individuals were free to affiliate with political parties of their own choice, The United Methodist Church never officially aligned itself with one political view or party; instead, its official stand was to support nationalism in a broad sense; nationalism that works for self-respect, dignity, and integrity for every person; nationalism that was not simply an exchange of masters, but one that worked toward genuine and total freedom and independence for the people of Zimbabwe as a whole.

Chapter 9

The Church and Its Urban Mission

The urban population in Zimbabwe is still quite small in comparison to that of the rural areas, yet the impact of urbanization and industrialization is noticeable. Consequently, more and more African people in Zimbabwe find their way to the city every year. Henry Makulu of Zambia depicted the situation graphically:

> The Africa of villages and the fast moving rivers and streams passing through thick, undisturbed forests and valleys is fast changing to the Africa of great metropolises, sites of hydro-electric dams, mines and modern factories . . . new towns are springing up all over Africa; large towns are growing larger.[1]

In this chapter, our discussion will have four foci: the origin of African migration to the city, the church in the city, The United Methodist Church in the city, and the theological foundation for the urban mission.

Origin of African Migration to the City

By 1931 only 39.3 percent of Zimbabwe's African male population was employed for wage labor in Zimbabwe. Roughly one-third of those men were employed in agriculture, another third in mining and the last third in other industries.[2] Again, according to J. Clyde Mitchell, there was a sharp rise of African men who were employed between the years 1931 through 1951; the percentage reached 68.3. As time went on, even as early as 1946, the number of African men in Zimbabwe employed in mining centers and on farms decreased, while the percentage of those employed in manufacturing (in cities) increased considerably. What attracted Africans to go and seek employment after 1931? While we may not have enough evidence to explain the sharp change that took place after 1931, at least we have some idea as to what may have contributed to the situation.

First, every African male in Zimbabwe was confronted with taxation. We have already noted that by 1924 The Methodist Episcopal Church was complaining to the government about the burden of the one pound poll tax that was required of male students who were in mission schools. Unless someone paid that tax for those students, they had to leave school for a while in order to earn the money to pay it. Taxation of African males was introduced in 1894, based on the idea that every African man should pay ten shillings "in respect of every hut which he occupied." Payments in crops, livestock (fowl, goat, cattle), or labor were acceptable for those who had no way of getting the money. By 1931 two shillings per head of cattle per year was also levied on cattle owners as a dipping fee. When the time came when taxation could be fulfilled only in currency and not in kind, the Africans were forced to accept the money economy by making their way to the city.

The second factor was the Land Apportionment Act (1931) which demanded the separation of white and black land.[3] This Act resulted in moving Africans from areas declared European. One can only speculate how much this added to that drastic change when many African males had to seek employment. Third, as Mitchell also points out, areas hit by droughts tended to be the places from where labor migration fluctuated with the success or failure of the crops. Finally, for parents who had realized the importance of educating their children, school fees had become a crucial issue. That led even more to the city.

All of this is to show that after Zimbabwe had been occupied by the white people a new way of life was introduced in the country, particularly in economics. With very little choice, the African had to accept a money economy by going to the city. Today Zimbabwe still has few beautiful, small cities, but does have several mining centers and numerous economic growth points, encouraged by the government since Independence, scattered all over the country.

Although agriculture has been the backbone of the economy of Zimbabwe for years, the manufacturing sector has grown rapidly. With the advent of Independence in 1980, the manufacturing sector contributed significantly toward the economic growth of the country. The growth in manufacturing was partly due to the removal of sanctions that crippled all efforts and the economy of Zimbabwe in the 1960s and 1970s.

With Independence in 1980, there was once again a great

increase of people in urban centers throughout Zimbabwe. This was because people wanted the expectations and dreams they had entertained for a long time under oppressive governments to be fulfilled. Of course, the same was even more true of those who had long left the rural areas because of the war of liberation that raged in the 1960s and 1970s. So we could say that both economic and political events throughout the country from the 1950s through the 1980s, or even to this day, attracted people to move to urban centers, including mining centers and the so-called growth points.

The Church in the City

Originally, churches in Zimbabwe found themselves in cities by comity agreements. Each denomination had its own exclusive area with the exception of the Roman Catholics who worked on their own. The end of World War II brought greater mobility in the country. Some young people traveled far from home to attend school. More men with their families went to the city and thus new problems with comity agreements arose. The churches felt obliged to follow their members, particularly those who moved to the city. In the city the Church found another kind of life to which to minister. What were some of the problems that Africans faced in cities and towns before Independence in 1980?

First, Africans were aliens in Southern Rhodesian cities to the extent that they had to get a permit to seek a job in the city. The assumption of the Land Apportionment Act was that the only reason an African had to be in the city was because he was working for a European. J. Clyde Mitchell is correct in pointing out that neither the government nor European employers took seriously African migration into the city:

> The type of housing, the social amenities and the wages of African workers seem to have been based on the assumption that they had come to the labor centers without their wives and families, who could support themselves by subsistence cultivation, and that their sojourn at the labor center in the meantime was temporary.[4]

Therefore, an African man's wage had never been thought of as supplanting, but rather as supplementing, subsistence cultivation in the tribal land. It was not until after Independence that for the first time the ZANU (PF) Government, by an Act of Parliament, genuinely tackled the problem and established the fact that Africans who were employed in urban areas, in mining centers, on farms, and as domestic labor had to be safeguarded by introducing a minimum wage. This was a recognition of the fact that other than their wages such employees had no other means of support.

The Land Tenure Act (1969) made things even worse. Africans lived in the city under one of the three categories: in African townships, in nonracial areas (which were very scarce), or with the appropriate permit at his place of employment. But all of this was conditional because "the appropriate government minister or local authority might, by notice in writing, prohibit the occupancy by Africans as outlined above."[5] That meant that every African in Rhodesian cities, then, was potentially in danger of being evicted from the area.

Second, housing continued to be one of the grave problems Africans had to face for years in Rhodesian cities. For Africans there were two categories of housing during colonial days: one scheme was administered by the municipalities whose program was basically rental. But the rent was extremely high for most of the residents. For example, in Mbare, then Harare Township, the municipality announced a monthly rent raise starting in November 1970, so that people who used to pay $2.90 began paying $15.00.[6] The complaint from tenants was that the houses were old and rotten. Three African workers were assigned to each room. Some of these workers were married and had families; the family members were not figured into the room allocation because the assumption was that nobody was supposed to bring a wife or children to those houses. A serious problem arose when wives lived in and raised children in these houses. The rooms were not large, most of them only seven feet by eleven feet,[7] and overcrowding was the result. The other scheme fell under advisory boards; this scheme encouraged home ownership by African people. But African areas were segregated from white areas, and of all the races in the cities, African houses were the most poorly constructed.

Third, there was the problem of transportation. It was the policy of white minority governments in Rhodesia to build African townships far away from the center of the city. To Africans this policy reflected the whites' fear of an African uprising. Naturally the distance made it hard on many African workers, especially for

124

those who could not afford the bus fare to go back and forth to work. Some companies provided their workers with money for bus fare; but who keeps money for bus fare when he has a hungry stomach? The only other alternatives were riding a bicycle or walking.

Finally, "poverty resulting in immorality" increasingly became a matter of concern in Rhodesian urban areas. Whether an African lived in the tribal trust lands or in the urban areas, however, poverty still remained one of the greatest enemies. In 1972, while the average salary for whites was $300 a month, on average the African wage was only $26 a month.[8] Who could decently feed and clothe a family on such wages? What plans could parents make for their children's education when they were so underpaid? Many men did not dare live with their families in the city; so the wife and family stayed in the tribal trust land. As a result, a lodger might be invited to occupy one of the few rooms. Often the lodger was a young man drawing an attractive salary; and if there were daughters growing up in the family problems were bound to arise. The young man, sympathetic to the plight of the family, would often assist them with food. The daughters would begin to visit his room and the mother of the house would quickly lose control of the situation.

The point of our illustrations is that the problems were not just urban problems. They had been built into structures; they were complicated by the political and economic philosophy of the minority white government called 'separate development.' This situation begs the questions: What did the churches in Rhodesia do about these problems? What did they understand to be their mission in the midst of the problems? In particular, what did The United Methodist Church do in its mission to urban areas?

Churches that started in the city, either by comity agreements before the 1920s, or later by following their members who had moved to the city during the 1930s and 1940s, continued to operate like rural congregations even though they were in the city. Regrettably, with some congregations the situation continued up to the 1970s. They perpetuated rural structures and a rural mentality dominated city churches too long to be effective in a quickly changing urban society. Henry Makulu's analysis was correct:

> Churches that have come into the urban centers have not been effective, because they are merely extensions of the village churches and because they have continued in village patterns, using village methods in their ministry to urban communities.[9]

An Evangelical Lutheran Church missionary, R. B. Schuyler found that church people in African cities, both pastors and laymen, were the most conservative people in maintaining village outlook on life. One of the reasons for this was the African ideal concept of the church which was very often "the mission station church." When church members went to the city, they considered their life and activities in the city as temporary and were not quick to transfer their membership (in the case of the United Methodists). So the village church, as the mission station church, for a long time dominated understanding of the nature of the church.

Furthermore, the attitudes of the missionaries toward the city for whatever reasons were not always as positive as they were toward mission stations. This was reflected in the amount of money appropriated to build and support urban churches in comparison with mission stations, particularly before the 1960s. The best preachers always found their way to mission-station churches rather than to urban areas. For a long time congregations existed in the cities but their ministry was taken for granted. Their growth was largely due to members moving in from village churches. By the 1960s, African churches in general in Rhodesia had to face the challenges of the city.

The most important dates in the history of Rhodesian churches in the city were 5–8 December 1968 when the first Rhodesian Urban Consultation was held in what was then Salisbury. Over 130 people attended the consultation from the four large cities and from most of the other centers coming from various denominations in the country, including the Roman Catholics. The speakers were invited from the United States of America, South Africa, Zambia, and Tanzania. Toward the end of the consultation, people were divided into groups and asked to discuss the kinds of things they wanted to see their churches doing in urban areas. Many ideas were collected and adopted by the joint planning committee. The things people wanted to see happen immediately were: (1) that every city and mining center form an urban church committee; (2) that each committee in every city seek ways to retrain and reorient their clergy and laity for urban ministry; (3) that in addition to evangelism and preaching, pastoral care and community involvement be given serious attention; (4) that churches review their programs and see what could effectively be done congregationally, denominationally, and ecumenically; (5) that churches explore the possibility of sharing their personnel, finances, and buildings to avoid unnecessary duplication. This was a great step for the churches in Rhodesia to enable themselves to look at urban mission together, seeking co-operation where possible. Indeed, the consultation was a success in bringing about a new awareness and desire to understand the complexity of the urban society, in order to engage in an effective ecumenical urban ministry. As far as structures were concerned, from 1968 the ministry of the Rhodesian churches in urban areas could be understood in the light of organizations that existed at three levels, interrelated and interdependent.

First, on the continental level, the Urban African Programme of the All Africa Conference of Churches came into existence in 1961 with a full-time secretary. It was affiliated with the Commission on World Mission and Evangelism of the World Council of Churches through the Urban and Industrial Mission from which most of the financial support came. Generally speaking, the purpose of the organization was to help African churches understand industrialization and urbanization. Most of the churches' projects that were tackled jointly or interdenominationally were coordinated through this organization in one way or another.

Second, on the national level, the Christian Council of Rhodesia in 1967 started the Urban Programme with a full-time secretary, Dr. Norman E. Thomas, a United Methodist Church missionary. Immediately, an advisory committee with representatives from all the four major cities in Rhodesia was formed; I served as its first chairman. The prime concern of the Urban Programme of the Christian Council of Rhodesia was to help create an atmosphere in which urban churches would be conscious of their existence as the Church of Christ Jesus in order to engage in an effective ministry by meeting needs of urban people. As a result of the 1968 Urban Church Consultation in Salisbury, churches in each one of the cities began to organize themselves for effective ministry in their individual cities. For example, while in Bulawayo the Council of Churches of Bulawayo was formed; in Salisbury it was the Salisbury Churches' Joint Action. The idea was for churches to look at their own city as a unit and to examine their resources of finances, personnel, and buildings, while trying to promote Christian understanding and unity in their respective urban areas.

United Methodism in the City

On the denominational level, by the late 1960s most churches in Rhodesia had become conscious of the need for an effective ministry in the cities. While this phenomenon was partially a result of interest in urban and industrial missions undertaken by their respective mother churches in Europe, North America, the United Kingdom, and others, at the same time the 1968 consultation in Salisbury was a great event that encouraged churches to take a fresh look at their work in the city and reorganize themselves for the challenges of urban mission.

Turning to The United Methodist Church, in 1969 a new committee was formed in the conference, the Board of Urban Ministries. The United Methodists who had given strong support to the 1968 Urban Consultation formed not only the Board of Urban Ministries but also a new urban district within the conference in 1969 in order to give special emphasis to urban development, with the Reverend Thomas Curtis as its first district superintendent. The prime concern of The United Methodist Church, whether through the Board of Urban Ministries or the new Urban District, was to fulfill God's mission in urban centers. Education of both the clergy and the laity in urban congregations became the most crucial issue. This was considered as providing means to urban congregations to become effective in meeting the needs of their people. The emphasis was on an ecumenical approach to urban ministry whenever possible. Today Christian worshipers can easily find a United Methodist congregation in most of the urban centers in Zimbabwe. That was certainly not the case before the 1960s due to the comity agreement which had restricted denominations in their respective areas.

Although The United Methodist Church came late to other urban centers like Harare, Bulawayo, Gweru, Masvingo, and others, its history of missionary work in Mutare is fascinating; and, as a matter of fact, its history is almost as old as the origin of the city itself. As indicated earlier, Morris Ehnes and his wife were the first Methodist Episcopal Church missionary couple to come to Southern Rhodesia. Arriving in October 1898, they immediately started both church and school work in the Mutare community. The establishment of a school for the white community in Mutare by The Methodist Episcopal Church was part of the agreement between the British South Africa Company and the Church through Bishop Hartzell. That agreement had stated that with the granting of the land by the former, the latter in return would provide education to children of the new white settlers. By 1901, the school, which became known as the Mutare Academy for children of the white settlers, had been established by the Church. The school included a chapel known as Saint Andrew's Methodist Episcopal Church. However, by 1909, the Mutare Academy had passed from church to government control; and since the missionary attitude then seemed to be that the Church's priority was to establish and concentrate its work among the African people, the Church welcomed the change.

Saint Andrew's, the chapel of the Mutare Academy, held an historic position in the life of United Methodism in Zimbabwe. It was the chapel where the first annual session of the East Central Africa Mission Conference was held on 16 November 1901. All along, the property of Saint Andrew's Church in Mutare was registered under The United Methodist Church and its predecessors until 1973 when both the congregation and the property were transferred to the Synod of the Methodist Church in Rhodesia.[10] The change came as a result of a motion passed by the Rhodesia Annual Conference of the Methodist Church in 1961. The situation was that while the annual conference provided pastoral appointment for Saint Andrew's Church, the congregation was primarily British and/or European. Indeed it was a white church where Africans were not welcome. Further, it is likely that white missionaries deliberately avoided association with the congregation for fear that they would be considered sympathizers of the racial attitudes that then prevailed.

Because the Rhodesian Methodist Synod had several white congregations in other urban centers, the Mutare Saint Andrew's Church presented their motion to the Rhodesia Annual Conference of the Methodist Church in 1961:

> The leaders of St. Andrew's Church, Umtali, at a meeting held on 15th March, 1961 unanimously agreed to request the Rhodesian Methodist Conference to approach the Rhodesian Methodist Synod in order that the Synod should take full responsibility for all aspects of the work at St. Andrew's: and that the details of the change-over of properties be gone into.[11]

The following year the board of trustees presented before the annual conference a two-fold recommendation that was approved:

(1) We considered the transfer of the St. Andrew's Church Building and Site, and the adjoining site now occupied by the Church Hall, from the Division of World Missions to the Methodist Synod. (2) We recommend that, after repayment of the William's loan on the St Andrew's Church Hall, the two sites and the Church Building be transferred, free of charge, to the Synod.[12]

The annual conference might not have looked beyond the "separate development" policy that ended with Independence in 1980. Wesley Church in Rusape, which also was a white congregation, left the Southern Rhodesia Annual Conference in a similar manner.

Reviewing the action taken by the annual conference, with all the historic attachments that the Southern Rhodesia Annual Conference originally had developed with Saint Andrew's Church as the place where history was created in the launching of United Methodism in this part of Africa, one feels as if the Southern Rhodesia Annual Conference of The United Methodist Church sold its birthright. I have no doubt in my mind as The United Methodist Church in Zimbabwe celebrates its centennial anniversary in 1997 that Saint Andrew's Church would have meant much more to them than it does to the Methodist Church in Zimbabwe.

It has already been pointed out that the Salisbury-Bulawayo District of the Rhodesia Annual Conference of The United Methodist Church was first organized in 1969 with special emphasis on a ministry whose main effort was to understand and meet the needs of people in urban and industrial areas of the country. However, in 1988, the Harare-Bulawayo District was split into two new districts; namely, Harare District and Masvingo-Bulawayo District. Today, Harare alone has two districts. This was to be expected because of the rapid growth and opportunities for expansion urban areas have in Africa today. These urban districts have challenges they need to face boldly. Indeed, no other districts in the conference have more opportunities or open doors set before them as a Christian community (Rev. 3:8) for effective evangelistic and pastoral work than do the urban districts.

First, the argument of pursuing one's members who have moved to urban areas because of employment opportunities is no longer sufficient explanation for a church's existence in an urban area.

The issue now is whether the Church is aggressive enough to penetrate all Zimbabwean urban centers in order to meet the spiritual, moral, and social needs of today's people. The task is too large for any one church to resort back to the comity argument.

Second, it is a historical fact that The United Methodist Church in Zimbabwe concentrated its work among African people. We have already noted that their work among white people did not really amount to anything significant. The question remains: Does it mean that post-Independence United Methodism still has no interest in people of other races? Or doesn't The United Methodist Church feel called to minister to people of other races other than the Blacks? Is the United Methodist Church going to be a racial church within a racially diverse or nonracial society? There may be no easy answers to the questions raised above. It may be easier to raise such questions than it is to provide solutions. However, The United Methodist Church would have to acknowledge the fact of the post-Independence era. How pleasing it is to see The United Methodist Church become so aggressive in its efforts to move beyond the townships and move on to the "First" or "Main" streets of our urban centers. The Church will likewise have to aggressively move on to suburbs and their shopping centers, for those are some of the places the Church will meet men and women who are influencing the nation's political and economic policies of today. And, indeed, such people also need the Church's ministry.

One might, in haste, say that The United Methodist Church is indeed meeting the challenge of the day. When one considers the growth rate at which United Methodism has taken its rightful place in urban centers, including establishing congregations in low density suburbs where they did not exist ten years ago, one cannot help recalling Jesus' words:

> The kingdom of heaven is like a mustard seed that someone took and sowed in his field; it is the smallest of all the seeds, but when it has grown it is the greatest of shrubs and becomes a tree, so that the birds of the air come and make nests in its branches (Matt. 13:30).

Theological Foundation for the Urban Mission

Social sciences have helped the Church in Africa to understand and bring into a much clearer focus the mission of the Church in

131

the cities. The Church's mission begins with God and therefore the theology of mission remains vitally important to the life of the Church. This is the reason why we find that in all urban consultations held in Africa theological presentations with biblical considerations are made, along with papers based primarily on findings of the social sciences. This rightly shows that the Church cannot rest with an awareness of social change; it needs a theology of that change, too. The question is: How has the Church in Africa looked at the city, in relation to its engagement in the urban mission?

As late as the 1980s, in Zimbabwe we were still talking of living in rural areas. This is the reason the Church in Africa has been so rural in its orientation. Mission stations trained people mainly to go to village churches and schools. African oral tradition depicted the city as destructive to their traditions and many Christians have maintained that attitude, whether they are in the city or in the village. It is not uncommon, even today, to hear a local church preacher refer to the city as Sodom and Gomorrah. Many people to this day would not even conceive of raising children in the city because they regard the city as an evil place. Yet, since independence, cities have absorbed more and more of our African people into their communities, and churches have every reason to be more involved in urban ministries. After all it is the modern person, the urbanized and industrialized person, who has the capacity and potential for leadership for the society of today. This has manifested the need for a more positive attitude and new theological reflection on the city if the Church is going to be meaningful at all in urban areas. With this in mind, we want to look at two factors: the city as a new creation, and the Church as a fellowship.

The City as a New Creation

Gibson Winter's idea of the city as a new creation seemed to catch the imagination of Africans in trying to understand theologically what was happening in the city in the 1960s. Winter wrote:

> Metropolis is the possibility of a unified, human society arising from the chaos of our massive, urbanized areas ... where children may find a climate conducive to growth, where education may enrich life as well as capacities, where men and women may have

opportunity to participate as members and receive their rewards, and where advantages may be distributed with equity.[13]

Dale White, of South Africa, who expounded this idea very convincingly in the 1960s, coupled Winter's "The New Creation (of God) as Metropolis" with Gerhard von Rad's interpretation of Genesis 2:4-24, where von Rad argues that creation was not finished until man 'named' the living creatures. Thus man becomes a co-worker in the creation process with God. As Dale White says, the city is God's new creation that needs God's people (the Church) to participate in it with proclamation and fellowship and service. By doing so they are involved in creation, through the ministry of redemption and fulfillment. If we are co-workers with God in the city that means we have a great responsibility. It means the influence of the Church should reach every aspect of urban life.

An additional challenge for the Church in urban areas was to develop a theology of work. Africans in Southern Africa generally looked at work in the city as exploitation and oppression by white people. How could they think otherwise, when, for example, in Zimbabwe during colonial days (as we have pointed out) a man's salary was racially based. Indeed, exploitation of one person by another in almost all sectors of the economy was rampant, and there was no standardized minimum wage yet. Post-Independence legislation, which raised the bargaining position of workers and democratized the decision making process by setting up workers' committees, helped to change people's attitude toward work. Africans began to feel that they belonged and that through their work they had a vital role to play in the development of their country.

While that change of attitude came about primarily through government legislation, churches throughout the country supported such efforts especially through ecumenical organizations like the Zimbabwe Council of Churches. That also meant that both government and churches became co-workers in the process of creating new life or new communities in urban Africa. If we think of the city as a new creation, then Egon Gerdes' theology of creation is helpful for it sheds light on what was happening in urban areas in Southern Africa during that period. His point is that the world is the meeting ground of God and humans; the world without the involvement of human beings becomes demonic or divinified; and without God the world becomes an object of exploitation by humans. Therefore the city as a new creation which seeks to fulfill the dreams and hopes of people in history should be the meeting place of God and people through His Church, in order for both to be involved in the act of creation, redemption, and fulfillment of human life.

The Church as a Fellowship

Adeolu Adegbola, for some time principal of Immanuel College, Ibadan, Nigeria, pointed out that "the Bible presents the Church to us not so much as an organization but as a community of faith in the fellowship of the Holy Spirit."[14] The phenomenon of the "house church" is common throughout Africa. The practice of these groups is to meet for prayer, Bible study, and discussion, and to learn of the problems and needs of their own community. While some of these groups are denominationally structured, others are ecumenical. Very often people who are not Christians but are interested in what goes on in these meetings are invited. The theological significance of the house church in Africa is that it represents Christianity at the grassroots of African community life. At that level the Christian faith attracts new converts by the way it is lived by members of the group.

There is something congenial to African traditional religion in the house church practice. After all, wasn't there a similar practice in the early Church? Paul informs us of the Church that met in the house of Prisca and Aquila (Rom. 16:5; 1 Cor. 16:19). Here the Church becomes the salt of the earth (Matt. 5:13) and the light of the world (Matt. 5:14), quietly and with little rhetoric; "It is like yeast that a woman took and mixed in with three measures of flour until all of it was leavened" (Luke 13:21). The Christian faith has been spreading in Africa in this way. Thus the Church has truly become a movement of the laity with little clericalization. This answers a need in the life of the Church in Africa when the ordained ministry equips the laity (Eph. 4:12).

A characteristic of United Methodist urban congregations is their division into a number of geographical sections. Each section has a leader, and each section has weekly meetings. That arrangement works well in enabling members of each congregation to get to know one another in their homes, to assist one another in case of death in the family, and to rejoice with one another in the case of events like weddings in the family.

Summary

(1) Initially, African men were reluctant to leave their traditional life in the rural areas for urban life; it was out of necessity that they eventually started moving to urban areas.

(2) During the colonial era, wages of African employees were based on the assumption that they had come to the labor centers without their wives and families, who were expected to support themselves by subsistence cultivation; their stay in town was understood as temporary.

(3) Originally churches in Zimbabwe found themselves in cities by comity agreements; each church was motivated to violate comity agreements by following its own members to new urban centers.

(4) Some of the problems that harassed Africans in urban centers were: housing, transportation, and poverty that sometimes resulted in immorality. In Rhodesia, churches rediscovered their urban mission in the 1960s and came up with both denominational and ecumenical programs to minister to people as best as they knew how.

(5) The United Methodist Church in Rhodesia launched an urban program by introducing an exclusively urban district in 1969; because of historical anomalies, United Methodism in urban centers is rapidly growing, not only in the high density areas, but also in the low density areas.

(6) Saint Andrew's Church in Mutare, which was a white congregation and the place where the first East Central Africa Mission Conference was organized in 1901, was handed over to the Methodist Church (originally from Britain) in Zimbabwe in the 1970s.

(7) While a number of people still hold to the view of cities as an evil place and as a place not meant for people to raise families, new theological reflection is also increasingly convincing people to see urban centers as God's new creation where God and his Church become co-workers, facilitating such urban centers as God's meeting ground with his people.

Chapter 10

The Church and Ecumenism

"Church unity and church renewal belong together as the work of the Holy Spirit. In this age, God is moving us to unity, not for its own sake, but for the mission."[1] This declaration of the Abidjan All-Africa Conference of Churches was readily adopted in 1970 by the Rhodesia Annual Conference of The United Methodist Church. In Africa, theological discussion on the unity or oneness of the Church in Christ Jesus has not always succeeded in convincing people. Yet once in a while, the challenge of the mission itself has convincingly indicated that the Church is one and ought to act as one.

Ecumenical relations are essential for the churches, for the oneness or unity of the Church in Christ Jesus is revealed as people work together. Ecumenism is never meant to be an end in itself; its thrust is to remind the churches in their sociological diversities that Christologically, the Church is one. Thus ecumenism enables the churches to understand themselves in the light of their common Christological nature, and to move obediently toward that oneness that is unveiled in Christ Jesus. The Church which is one in Christ Jesus becomes so in history, with mission as its conscience.[2]

Thus, when missionaries in Southern Rhodesia organized the first interchurch body, the Southern Rhodesia Missionary Society, in January 1904, it was through the challenge of mission that they realized the need for one another. By drawing together they were involved in ecumenical relations. This chapter seeks to show how the United Methodists, together with other churches, have been involved in ecumenical relations primarily in Zimbabwe during the post-World War II period. In what follows, three main points will focus our discussion: national interchurch bodies, unity talks, and theological education.

National Interchurch Bodies

There were two main national interchurch bodies in Zimbabwe during the 1950s and the 1960s: the Rhodesia Christian Conference and the Zimbabwe Christian Council, now the Zimbabwe Council of Churches. The United Methodist Church and its predecessors were members of those two interchurch bodies until 1971, when the Rhodesia Annual Conference decided to withdraw its membership from the Rhodesia Christian Conference.

The Rhodesia Christian Conference

The Rhodesia Christian Conference was originally known as the Missionary Society, and then, for a time, as the Southern Rhodesia Missionary Conference. It was primarily missionary oriented; that is, the organization approached issues as missionaries did. The organization started in 1904 in Bulawayo with the purpose of mutual intercession and cooperation, especially in evangelism and Christian education. Time and again, their mission demanded their cooperation; for example, missionaries in Rhodesia found that they needed one another in facing difficulties in their work, dealing with government officials, working on Bible translations, handling the comity agreements, and many other things. Because the Southern Rhodesia Missionary Conference was a missionary organization, the Southern Rhodesia Bantu Christian Conference was established in 1928, with the approval of the former.[3] The African organization was prohibited from discussing the constitution of any of the churches that were represented, or any financial or other arrangements. Since the president of the missionary conference was also the chairman of the Bantu Christian Conference, an introduction of such items into discussion could easily be ruled out of order.

Missionaries were interested in cooperation, but their cooperation was naturally based on the problems and issues that they faced as a missionary body. They were not necessarily thinking in terms of the Church or about problems African leaders faced as blacks. African leaders, who could have raised embarrassing questions (for example, about the obvious disunity among Christians) had to be restricted. In other words, the cooperation of missionaries was limited and African leaders were restricted to peripheral issues.

138

Professor T. O. Ranger, in his study on state and church in Southern Rhodesia, has demonstrated that the missionary conference became a strong political power in the 1920s. Most of its meetings were attended by government officials. After the experience of World War I, the 1920s presented a threatening issue to the white government in Southern Rhodesia and the white population at large, namely racial equality. For example, following World War I the Southern Rhodesian government's attitude toward American missionaries was cold. It was feared that American missionaries were going to educate the African to the level of the British ruler. There was also the fear that American missionaries would inform Africans about the social equality of blacks and whites in America. Above all it was feared that the African American was ready to return to Africa. Walter Aiden Cotton had published a book, *The Race Problem in South Africa*, in which he encourage mixed marriages. On 2 December 1926 the chief "Native" commissioner of Southern Rhodesia wrote in reply:

> To put into the heads of the natives misleading and dangerous notions of social equality is a doctrine which cannot in all decency be permitted . . . and a native is a native and will always remain, no matter to what state of civilized advancement he may achieve. . . .[4]

With all those fears rampant in the 1920s it is remarkable that the voice of the missionary conference in Southern Rhodesia was heard at all. In 1924 the government of Southern Rhodesia decided to draft a bill which sought to control and regulate African preachers in their teachings and preaching.[5] The missionary conference resisted the bill and it was dropped.[6] Also, when the 1923 constitution gave the white population self-government with no representation for the African people at all, it was partly through the efforts of the Southern Rhodesia Missionary Conference that two whites had to be elected to represent African interests.[7] The most influential personalities in this struggle were Arthur Cripps, an Anglican missionary, and John White, who was then chairman of the Methodist Synod in Southern Rhodesia. John White was a member of the conference executive body almost without a break between 1920 and 1930, and from 1924 through 1928 he was president.

The 1920s are unique in the history of the Southern Rhodesia Missionary Conference. In the form of the Rhodesia Christian

Conference in the 1950s and 1960s, the organization had refused to be involved in political issues at all. Its members would not even talk about unity, and for that reason were not enthusiastic about the World Council of Churches. The organization was inclined to perceive evangelism and politics as diametrically opposed to each other. Therefore, while they would support any program that dealt with evangelism, they always retreated when it came to political issues. Theologically speaking, the Rhodesia Christian Conference was steadily getting out of step with the thinking of the emerging African leadership in the Church in the 1960s. Consequently, most of its staunch supporters were among the strong conservative element of the Church.

The Zimbabwe Christian Council

The Zimbabwe Christian Council, which came into existence early in the 1960s, became an Associate Council of the World Council of Churches. Its style of ecumenical relations was different in emphasis. To begin with, the Zimbabwe Christian Council was constituted by churches (as opposed to missionaries) which sought to face issues that came up as the Church of Christ Jesus. There was a conscious attempt among these churches to negotiate for union. This was the reason why the Rhodesia Annual Conference of the Methodist Church charged its own committee to the Zimbabwe Christian Council with the task of actively investigating possibilities of union with other churches.

The theological ferment of the Zimbabwe Christian Council was different from that of the Rhodesia Christian Conference. For example, the Church was no longer understood as being denominational. The understanding of the Church went beyond sociological limits. There was a willingness in the Council to search for and face the theological meaning of the Church. Salvation was no longer understood only in the sense of evangelistic efforts that end with conversion; rather, there was more interest in the whole person, his personal as well as his social life. This meant involvement in the social and political life of Rhodesia, as well as in special projects that helped humanize the African in the country, who, under white supremacy, had been dehumanized in many ways.

The United Methodist Church in Rhodesia took a very keen interest in the program of the Zimbabwe Christian Council. It withdrew its membership from the Rhodesia Christian Conference in order to give all its support to the Christian Council. The United Methodist Church also furnished trained personnel to head some of the departments of the council. For example, in 1966 Abel T. Muzorewa, now retired bishop of The United Methodist Church in Zimbabwe, served as the Council's youth secretary until his election to the episcopacy in 1968. Also, Norman Thomas, now a professor in the United States and former lecturer at Epworth Theological College, served as the Council's secretary of urban evangelism from 1968 until 1971. The establishment of the Zimbabwe Christian Council toward the end of the 1960s was a refreshing and renewing experience in the life of the Church in Rhodesia. It strengthened the Church and gave it hope as it battled with hostile political and economic policies of the day.

Unity Talks

The United Methodist Church in Rhodesia took the matter of unity seriously, particularly in the 1960s. It constantly reminded itself that it was pressing for organic union with other churches in the country. Unity talks of the United Methodist Church were going on at three levels: Interchurch conversations for unity within Methodism, Union within Methodism, and unity talks with the United Church of Christ.

Interchurch Conversations for Unity

The year 1968 for a while stood as a milestone in the efforts of churches in Rhodesia that pursued conversations for unity. The following churches stated publicly at various times that they agreed to pursue the call to unity: the Anglican Dioceses of Mashonaland and Matebeleland, the United Congregational Church of Southern Rhodesia, the Rhodesia Annual Conference of The United Methodist Church, the Methodist Church in Rhodesia and the Rhodesia Presbyteries of the Presbyterian Church of South Africa. We will briefly touch on each of the five statements released in 1968 ("On Calling to Unity," "A Statement of Common Belief," "On the Ministry," "On Organic Union," and "On the Covenant"), before we try to comment on them as a whole.

141

First, *"On Calling to Unity"* (adopted November 1966): In 1968, the churches that participated in the conference reaffirmed their belief that the Holy Spirit was calling them from the diversities of their traditions to be strengthened in fellowship with the hope of eventual organic union, so that in a renewed spiritual power they might together face their apostolic task.

Second, *"A Statement of Common Belief"* (adopted June 1967): The statement of agreed belief includes only what the churches agreed upon; their disagreements are not included. It was agreed however, that what they did not agree upon was to receive further examination and discussion. This statement touches on a number of things: (1) the summons to unity; (2) the gospel of God's grace; (3) the authority of Scripture; (4) the relation of Scripture to the tradition of the Church; (5) one, holy, catholic and apostolic Church; (6) ministry in the Church; (7) the sacraments of Baptism and the Lord's Supper; and (8) the Kingship of Christ.[8]

Third, *"On the Ministry"* (adopted January 1968): It was affirmed that God has owned and blessed the existing ministries of the uniting churches as true ministries of His word and sacraments, (notwithstanding some remaining barriers to intercommunion). It was agreed to have only one form of ministry in the United Church. It was further agreed, that, should the bishops be within the historic succession, no one particular interpretation of the origin or transmission of the Christian ministry could be insisted upon with the United Church. Incorporation into the United Church of the values that had been preserved and maintained for the Church Universal by the eldership of the Presbyterian Church, the emphasis on lay-preaching in the Methodist Church, and the Meeting of Churches of the Congregational form of government, were to be considered.

Fourth, *"On Organic Union"* (adopted January 1968): The goal of the conversations was clearly spelled out as organic union. Organic union meant that the uniting churches would be brought to a stage when they would dissolve their present constitutions in favor of a new one. Valuable emphases from uniting churches would be preserved, but there had to be room for the new that comes with organic union as a living faith.

Finally, *"On the Covenant"* (adopted January 1968): A Covenant had to be made by churches in order to establish, crystallize, and demonstrate to the whole Church the seriousness of the purpose of the participating churches. The Covenant service was to be arranged no later than Pentecost 1970. After the Covenant was over, participating churches were to establish a consultative council for the discussion and promotion of matters of common concern, and so pave the way for the day of inauguration of union. The Covenant was summed up in the following words:

> (1) to seek agreement on a complete statement of common belief; (2) to seek agreement on such a form of oversight and ministry; and (3) to admit to the Lord's Table baptized communicant members of all our churches as an immediate and visible sign of our fellowship, and the earnest of full communion to come.

The Covenant service was not carried out as planned because the Anglican Diocese of Mashonaland did not agree with the original draft of the Covenant. Instead of the intercommunion they suggested occasional services where ministers of all churches would participate. Other churches would not accept the amendment proposed by the Anglicans. Nevertheless, working committees were called for to (1) prepare a draft constitution for a United Church; (2) consider the formation of a trust for joint holding of properties; and (3) plan for a lay conference on church unity. Unfortunately it all came to nothing.

With the rejection of intercommunion services by the Anglican Diocese of Mashonaland the unity conversations lost momentum in the 1970s. Not only did nothing significant happen after the rejection of intercommunion services; in addition, the acknowledgement of collapse of unity talks by the six major denominations in the country was reported at the Rhodesia Annual Conference of The United Methodist Church by its ecumenical relations committee in 1978.

At this point we pause for theological reflection about the progress that unity talks among churches of Rhodesia made between 1966 and 1970. First, the churches of Rhodesia were conscious of the sociological need for organic union. Several causes may have contributed. Mother churches overseas were involved in unity talks and these were the main issue in other African countries too. Furthermore, the political climate in the country had become a threat to the Church as an institution. Thus institutional survival influenced the motivation of unity talks, particularly in a time when funds from abroad were being cut. Naturally, the exact nature of the situation was at that time an object for speculation.

Second, while the Rhodesian churches had been willing to cooperate on the social level there was unfortunately a suppression of theological issues. This can be illustrated by two incidents from the report. (1) After parading what the churches agreed upon with one another, nothing in the report states their differences. It might have been good strategy to emphasize the positive aspect of the ecumenical efforts, but genuine union can hardly grow without openness with one another. Without openness, members of each tradition would not be enabled to understand and appreciate the theological position of the other church. In fact, newness can emerge only with the new understanding and appreciation that comes with the unveiling of the diversity of traditions represented by participating churches. The refusal of the Anglican Diocese of Mashonaland to go ahead with the plan of intercommunion hurt many because theologically only a few were prepared for it. Theological issues were allowed to lag behind sociological concerns.

(2) It was agreed that if the personal oversight of bishops was to be within the historic succession, no one particular interpretation of the origin or transmission of the Christian ministry could be insisted upon for the United Church. Certainly, theological pluralism within the old traditional positions held by the uniting churches was the most pragmatic way to proceed. But pragmatism does not help to answer the question: What were the options? Yet the churches were reluctant to go into this issue, although it is only in the act of each church divulging its theological differences in the midst of sympathetic partners that genuine integration and spiritual renewal could occur. Now that unity conversations had collapsed among the churches of Rhodesia, maybe they could have taken time for reflection.

As one who was involved in some of the conversations, though only for a brief period, I can make certain observations. First, the church unity talks in Rhodesia attracted a high level of white representation. Most of those whites came to the talks with the background of churches as they knew them from their own different countries: America, Europe, Great Britain, Australia, South Africa, and others. I am not saying that if unity talks representation had been black then organic union would have been reached easily; as a matter of fact, that would have been another problematic issue.

But we have to recognize the existence of a problem with representatives dominated by white expertise in churches engaged in the African mission.

Second, the issues that churches agreed to discuss were traditional rather than doctrinal and about order rather than faith. There seemed to be deliberate avoidance of theological discussion on issues that churches shared in common or which divided them by a number of leaders, possibly in order to make sure that they preserved their tradition and order. Although by this time more and more Africans were articulating their theological positions, the problem was often whether their views would find support from their church hierarchy.

Third, the African Church hierarchy, whether it be white or black, needs to start thinking about the Church more theologically rather than simply ecclesiastically. The time has come for the Church in Africa to raise questions with which it needs to wrestle. For example: What is the Church? What is the nature of God's mission for the Church in Africa? What is unity? What kind of unity does the Church in Africa seek? What is the relationship between mission and unity? Is it organic unity or something else that churches are pursuing? What options are there? In what areas in the life of the Church are we already experiencing the spirit of unity? These and many other questions should be encouraged by leaders, especially by those in the church hierarchy.

Finally, the commonality of African culture and tradition should help bring about a united human voice in the churches of Africa to answer the voice of Christ. Unfortunately the African church finds itself increasingly divided by foreign cultures and traditions that have no relevance to God's mission on the continent.

Union within Methodism

On 26 January 1962, a meeting was held at the request of Bishop Ralph Dodge. The meeting was between the African Methodist Episcopal Church, the Synod of the Methodist Church in Southern Rhodesia, and the Southern Rhodesia Annual Conference of what is now The United Methodist Church. They all agreed to work toward union but the African Methodist Episcopal Church never attended any subsequent meetings.

The synod of the Methodist and the annual conference of the

United Methodist Churches met consistently every year and had also cooperated in many projects, but did not come to a point where they could talk about organic union. Two problems frustrated fruitful conversations. First, there was the old arrangement of missionaries, namely, comity agreements. According to that arrangement, Salisbury, Bulawayo, and Gweru, the three largest cities in Zimbabwe, were within the jurisdiction of the synod whilst Mutare, the fourth largest city, was the only one that fell within the jurisdiction of the conference. That was workable as long as Southern Rhodesia was still primarily rural. By 1932 the annual conference of the Methodist Church realized that there were about nine hundred of their members in Salisbury. The agreement between the Methodist churches was to take care of the members of each other's church when they happened to be in each other's area. With so many members of the Methodist Church (conference) in Salisbury the solution to the problem proved to be difficult. The appointment of a Methodist Church (conference) pastor, Josiah Chimbadzwa to Salisbury from 1941 to 1946 under the supervision of the Methodist Church (synod), to take care of both groups of Methodists, did not work as a solution. After Josiah Chimbadzwa left Salisbury in 1946 there was more pressure from the Methodist (conference) members in Salisbury for a pastor of their own, and also for a place of their own where they could worship freely. The Methodist Church (conference), desiring to keep the comity agreements and not embarrass their Methodist brethren or jeopardize their relationships with the Methodist Church (synod), resisted the pressure. The unfortunate result was that the Independent Church came into existence in the year 1949. A first group had broken away from the Methodist Church in 1932, as we indicated earlier. This was the second breakaway movement.

For fear of other breaks with other groups in other cities, The United Methodist Church moved into all urban areas in the country. By January 1969 a new urban district was formed in the conference. As far as the Methodist Church was concerned, this meant ignoring comity agreements and it hurt conversations for union. In 1969 the Rhodesia Annual Conference of The United Methodist Church accounted for its move in the following statement:

(1) We are two separate denominations who are in close fellowship with each other due to our common Wesleyan heritage.

(2) The geographical division of Rhodesia between our two churches (comity agreement), although useful in the past when workers were few and the population lived largely in rural areas, can no longer be the guide for the working relationships between our churches. (3) The movement of large numbers of both denominations into the towns requires the expansion of both our churches with them.[9]

This statement provoked discussion lasting a whole afternoon with the Methodist Church (Synod) questioning the emphasis on the "two separate denominations." Since then there has not been any more meaningful or profitable discussion on the subject between the two sister churches.

The second problem in the way of inter-Methodist conversations was the tendency to discuss projects or areas of cooperation without theological engagement. Little guidance has been given in discussions frustrated or hindered by the two traditions of Methodism, namely, British and American. As much as these traditions are essential to Methodism in Africa, it is essential that their ecclesiastical traditions be kept in dialogue with Wesleyan theology.

For quite some time, the two Methodist Churches had tried to cooperate in a number of projects and programs especially in the cities. For example, they have always shared church buildings if the other one was in need; and in some high density areas this arrangement went as far as jointly erecting church buildings. However, it must be pointed out immediately that this has not been done without some painful difficulties! Some of the difficulties connected with such joint projects of church buildings have managed to bring efforts and plans to nothing. It was disappointing in 1977 to receive a report at the annual conference that one of the congregations had pulled out of such joint projects.[10]

While desires for disunity are easily and openly expressed at the grassroots level it is not easy to determine how many similar attitudes there are among the church hierarchy. What is obvious is that while the need for unity may be demonstrated from the top, the desire to discontinue such programs has often been expressed from the grassroots. Probably this shows us that as much as unity is essential for the community of Christ, guidance and instruction are also necessary for our people. It might be that the church leadership has failed to prepare people for the essential values that are preached. These experiences of working and worshiping to-

147

gether as sister churches provide an opportunity and raw material for genuine and relevant theological reflection. It means that people talk out of their community experience.

Unity Talks with The United Church Of Christ

United Methodist Church talks with the United Church of Christ in Zimbabwe started in 1969. Some of the subjects that were discussed were: (1) government of the Church; (2) organization of the local Church; (3) types and qualifications of the ministry; (4) forms of worship and sacraments; (5) special theological viewpoints; (6) standards for church membership; (7) rules and discipline of members; (8) ethos, that is, the distinctive character of our churches and fellowships; (9) land and properties; (10) finance; (11) areas of joint action; and (12) personnel.

From the start, the participants were amazed at how much the two churches had in common. However, there were areas of friction. Policies regarding smoking stood out very clearly as one of them. While the United Church of Christ members are permitted to smoke, both clergy and laity of The United Methodist Church in Zimbabwe are not. This is an item that the United Methodists have to face at all levels when they pursue conversations for unity. Other areas that needed further exploration were the government of the church, the organization of the local church, and infant baptism.

In 1970 the Zimbabwe Annual Conference decided to send the results of these discussions to local churches, and the United Church of Christ did the same thing. The idea was to have local churches involved, letting them raise the necessary questions. Arrangements were to be made to get different groups to discuss issues from their particular vantage point. Again, all came to nothing.

As a participant in the first two meetings between The United Methodist Church and the United Church of Christ, I must say the meetings were remarkably congenial. One is tempted to say that the spirit in which the meetings were conducted suggested that there was no barrier that could not be overcome. One reason for the kind of spirit that prevailed seemed to be that both churches had an American background. This has made some of us think that the difficulties that have frustrated The United Methodist Church and The Methodist Church unity talks were compounded by a failure to reconcile the American and British ecclesiastical traditions.

Another factor that was noticeable in the unity talks at all levels was the lack of participation by the African clergymen. The discussions were dominated by missionaries who still looked at the Church through Western eyes, or through the traditions from which they came. African ministers attended meetings, but the missionaries who had the advantage of better training remained authorities in both ecclesiastical and theological issues. Naturally this raises a question: To what extent did the unity talks represent African interest and experience? This question might trouble us for a few more years.

Theological Education

One of the main elements in the life of the Church in Africa particularly since the late 1950s has been the area of theological education. Because our main interest in this book is The United Methodist Church in Zimbabwe, we will look at two factors in its theological education enterprise based at the United Theological College: theological education in relationship to general higher education and the relevance of theological education.

First, let us turn to theological education in relationship to general higher education. As early as 1917 a committee of the Southern Rhodesia Mission conference of the Methodist Episcopal Church and the Wesleyan Methodist Church reached an agreement to train their ministers together.[11] However, the merger of theological training of pastors by the two Methodist churches did not take place until 1959 at Epworth Theological College.

In 1956 the Methodist Church (synod) in Zimbabwe decided to move their theological training college from Waddilove Mission to Epworth Mission, near what is now Harare. The new college became known as Epworth Theological College. Similarly, The Methodist Church (conference), through negotiations with The Methodist Church (synod), decided to move the theological training of their pastors from Hartzell Theological Seminary at Old Mutare in order to be in a joint effort with The Methodist Church (synod) at Epworth Theological College in 1959. I was one of the pioneer students of the joint venture. Other churches joined the two Methodist Churches in training their pastors at Epworth Theological College. The United Church of Christ in Zimbabwe joined in 1961; the Evangelical Lutheran Church in 1965; and the United Congregational Church of Southern Africa in 1969. The Anglican Church and the Presbyterian Church had each sent students to Epworth from time to time to participate in the education without however becoming members of the College. Although the other churches participated in the Theological College Council, officially the college was under the control of the two Methodist churches who had the right to nominate a candidate for the principalship. It was not until 1972 that a new constitution was approved which gave equal power to all participating churches.[12] That constitution made Epworth Theological College an interdenominational theological college; and eventually the name of the college changed to the United Theological College.

During the same time there was interest in establishing theological colleges close to government-sponsored universities that were growing in Africa. The advantages were that the theological colleges would share the staff of theological faculties of universities where such faculties were established, and that the university environment enabled cross-fertilization of ideas through the use of university libraries and the exposure to international scholars.[13] The head of the department of religious studies of Ibadan University warned the Church to guard herself against the myth of advantage of moving near a university. His argument was that university departments of theology and religion could at times be headed by scholars of other faiths, like Islam; others feared that university relations would result in dependence upon the university.

For the United Theological College the crucial issue was not necessarily the moving to the physical proximity of a university; rather, it was the question of constitutional relationships of the theological college with the university. The United Theological College is about sixteen kilometers from the University of Zimbabwe. There was an appreciation for the advantages and good arguments favoring this theological college because of its relationships with a university for higher academic training for the ministry of the Church. Yet the need was felt for the Church to retain its independence in theological training in order to fulfill the goals of theological education it had set for itself. The idea was that qualified students at the United Theological College should be able to take divinity subjects in the department of theology at the university, supplemented by other subjects at the United Theological College, enabling the students to graduate with a B.A. in theology;[14] so far this relationship has not been established. In 1972 the United Theological College presented an application to become an associate college of the university but the application was declined.

However, a new working relationship between the United Theological College and University of Zimbabwe Department of Religious Studies, Classics, and Philosophy was eventually agreed upon. The University of Zimbabwe designed a three-year theological course leading to a diploma in religious studies. Qualified students can follow the diploma studies at the University, while the remaining part of their syllabus is covered at the United Theological College. Successful students graduate with both the University of Zimbabwe diploma in religious studies, and the Theological College diploma.

Another factor that contributed significantly toward theological education in Africa was the Theological Education Fund which was started in 1958. The fund was made available to theological colleges where churches were willing to train their ministers together. The main thrust of the fund has been to raise standards of scholarship in ministerial training in the Third World. The fund helped theological colleges in many ways; funding, for example, common textbooks, library programs, theological staff institutes, and scholarships. In 1964 the United Theological College also received some help from the fund.

Thus various factors came together to help churches with the training of ministers. This was important in a situation where churches were engaged in conversations for union. For example, there are between seven and ten churches that send their students to the United Theological College in Zimbabwe. In addition to the exposure students and staff have in the college community, churches are also involved in constant dialogue and fellowship through the college council. This allows for a new acceptance of one another as a direct result of daily or frequent acquaintance.

However, a point to remember is that the Church in Africa should never lose sight of the fact that theological education is for the whole Church; and that it is never meant to be restricted to clericalized ministry alone. It is meant to equip the whole Church in order to engage in the ministry of Christ (Eph. 4:12). While theological colleges should do all they can to enable students to mature intellectually, spiritually, and morally, ultimately theological education needs to be felt in the whole ministry of the Church—both among clergy and laity.

Summary

(1) Time and again the Church has stood up fearlessly to defend human rights when governments decided otherwise. That was the case in the 1920s and early 1930s as the Southern Rhodesia Missionary Conference enjoyed the influential leadership of missionaries like Arthur Cripps and John White.

(2) As they had in the mainstream denominations elsewhere, such as in West Africa, East Africa, and overseas, unity talks among the denominations of Zimbabwean churches failed in the 1960s and 1970s. It would be helpful for the Church in Zimbabwe to set up a special committee to study the reasons why such unity talks failed before more effort is made to resume the exercise. Ideally, this should apply at all levels of relationships at which such negotiations were taking place.

(3) Theological education in Zimbabwe has benefited from and generated a spirit of renewal and cooperation among churches. One hopes that this forward-looking response on the part of churches continues until the search for union leads to realization.

Chapter 11

The Church During the War of Liberation

In 1964 Rhodesia's white leaders, the Rhodesia Front, decided to take a sharp ideological turn to the right, moving closer to South Africa's policy of apartheid in their relationship with the blacks of Rhodesia. This did not come as a surprise to many blacks, for they knew that the white leaders then were thoroughly oriented toward white South Africa; hence, on 11 November 1965, the Unilateral Declaration of Independence (UDI). Again, it was clear to anyone following the sequence of events in Southern Africa at the time that the main motivation for UDI was the preservation and entrenchment of white rule in Rhodesia. Equally important, in May 1964 the Zimbabwe African National Union (ZANU) Congress which was held in Gweru had resolved to renounce all further negotiations with the white Rhodesian leaders; instead they advocated to pursue the armed struggle.

This was not the first time that blacks of Rhodesia had overtly sought to defy their rulers in a war so that they could liberate themselves. As a matter of fact, their first war of liberation had been in 1896–97 soon after the occupation of the country by the whites in 1890. Among the chief characters resisting white rule and mobilization of the masses into war were Sekuru (Uncle) Kaguvi and Mbuya (Grandma) Nehanda in Mashonaland, and Chief Chingaira Makoni in Manicaland, to mention just three. While Chingaira Makoni was a chief, Kaguvi and Nehanda were mediums of *mhondoro* (royal ancestral spirits). As mediums, their message was simple and clear, namely that all white men must be killed without mercy, "Preaching war to the finish."[1] Although the first uprising was quickly quelled, resulting in the execution of Sekuru Kaguvi, Mbuya Nehanda, Chief Makoni, and many others, still there remained tension throughout the land.

In addition, the decision by the Rhodesia Front and ZANU

153

parties in 1964 formalized a hostile relationship between the blacks and whites in the land. As a matter of fact, such decisions were preparation for another confrontation and war.

The War of Liberation

The Chinhoyi Battle in Mashonaland West, on Friday, 28 April 1966, has often been regarded as the beginning of the second war of liberation in Rhodesia.[2] For the first time, the myth that blacks would never take up arms against their white bosses, which had until then been comfortably believed by most Rhodesian whites, was dismissed. Although the seven young men who belonged to the Zimbabwe African National Liberation Army (ZANLA, the military wing of ZANU) were all killed in the battle, it became an important military experience for ZANLA. It was from the Chinhoyi Battle that ZANLA, after reflection on what had happened there, adopted a new strategy whose emphasis was to infiltrate the masses in the communal lands so that ZANLA would be able to mobilize and politicize the people while at the same time avoiding confrontation with the white security forces where possible. And it was also out of this successful political and military infiltration into the masses by ZANLA that the young people who had been termed "terrorists" by the Rhodesia Front regime through a countrywide propaganda became regarded as "freedom fighters" by the masses. As a result, the masses provided shelter and food to their freedom fighters as well as protecting the young men and women from their enemy.

By 1972, through intensive ground work and politicization of the masses, ZANU opened the eastern military operations front that surprised the white settlers. White farmers in the areas were attacked; military vehicles that went into the area to relieve farmers were blown up by landmines; and the freedom fighters were even capable of firing rockets and other weapons from a safe distance.[3] In September 1974, after Portugal had handed over the reins of power in Mozambique to the Front for the Liberation of Mozambique (FRELIMO), full independence followed in June 1975. Such an action of withdrawal from Mozambique by Portugal marked the beginning of a vital military operational front for ZANU to cross the border and infiltrate further into Rhodesia. It was not long before vast areas became "no-go areas" having fallen under the complete control of the freedom fighters.

ZIPRA (Zimbabwe Peoples' Revolutionary Army), the military wing of ZAPU (Zimbabwe African Peoples' Union), had Zambia as its base. It recruited young people both from Rhodesia and from those who were already in Zambia. They claimed to use both conventional and guerrilla methods of warfare.[4]

As the security forces of the white regime in Rhodesia responded to the new situation, which obviously seemed beyond their control, a number of drastic measures were taken in an attempt to control movement of people in the communal lands and crossing of border into Mozambique. For instance, people were removed from their homes, leaving their houses, furniture, cattle, goats, and fields to rot. The people were crowded in places known as "keeps" or "protected villages." A curfew system was introduced and brutally enforced. Curfew violaters were killed without mercy. Ken Flower points out that between 1964 and 1974 white Rhodesians were in a winning position, as far as the war was concerned; from 1972 to 1976 they had entered a "no-win" war; and after 1976 they were fighting a losing war.[5]

Having realized that they were losing the war at home, the white leaders yielded to the clamor amongst the whites to extend the war across the Rhodesia borders. First, on 9 August 1976, the Rhodesia Army used its Selous Scouts Group and invaded Nyadzonia base in Mozambique where large numbers of unarmed and untrained people were killed.[6] Second, on 23 December 1977, ZANLA camps at Chimoio and Tembue in Mozambique were attacked by the white Rhodesians; about two thousand people were killed.[7] Between 18 and 20 October 1978, the ZIPRA camp at Chikumbi, near Lusaka, was stormed by the white Rhodesian army; about sixteen hundred people were killed.[8]

These raids across the border were successful insofar as they made life miserable for the freedom fighters and made leaders of the two countries encourage an end to the war. But those freedom fighters who were in the field—fighting inside Rhodesia—never lost sight of the victory which was to be theirs.

While the Rhodesian soldiers concentrated on crossing the borders into Zambia and Mozambique, the freedom fighters concentrated on crossing borders into Rhodesia and held firmly to whatever land they brought under their control. By 1976, several white farmers fled from their farms and went to the cities; the blacks who were in urban areas ceased their frequent weekend trips to the

155

communal land because the war had taken a new dimension. Indeed, the freedom fighters were in control of vast areas in the communal lands.

It was sad for the people in the communal land for they found themselves caught between the white regime's army and the freedom fighters. While the Rhodesian army murdered several leaders in the communal land, including politicians, pastors, teachers, visitors from urban areas, and many others, freedom fighters killed white farmers, Rhodesian soldiers, and blacks who chose to collaborate with the white regime; at times, for reasons they alone knew. Needless to say, many innocent people from both sides were killed in that war. By 1978 it was believed that about two thousand people were being killed each month.

Several attempts were made to resolve the Rhodesia crisis through negotiations: in the Anglo-Rhodesian negotiations aboard HMS Tiger in 1966; another talk aboard HMS Fearless in 1968; the Victoria Falls Conference between the Rhodesian Government and Nationalists leaders set up by President Kenneth Kaunda of Zambia and Prime Minister John Vorster of South Africa in 1971; and the Anglo-American initiative which led to the Geneva Conference in 1976. In spite of all those efforts to bring about a settlement to the Rhodesia crisis, none transpired.

The Church in Rhodesia

Many church leaders, both lay and ordained, lost their lives during the war. In fact, anybody who held a position of leadership, especially in the communal lands, was liable to face death at any time. I recall attending a funeral of a United Methodist pastor and his wife, Elisha and Tamary Kuwana, who had both been brutally murdered by the Rhodesia security forces. On another occasion I confronted the security forces after they shot a young United Methodist pastor, Thomas Mvenge, who was trying to stop some of the government security forces from aimlessly beating people in a "keep." It was a rule of terror.

Some of the worst atrocities by the Rhodesian security forces were the killings of the local people in order to discredit the liberation movement. As a result, in February 1977, seven Catholic missionaries were allegedly murdered by guerrillas at Saint Paul's Mission.[9] In June 1978, thirteen British missionaries and children at Elim Pentecostal Mission in Penhalonga, near Mutare, were massacred. All this was done by the Selous Scouts as an effort by the Rhodesian regime, which realized how isolated it had become, in order to draw support from Western countries by slaying missionaries. Two persons who deserted from the Selous Scouts are said to have since testified to the fact.[10] Such were the tactics by a people who claimed that they had a special mission in Southern Africa to preserve Christianity and Western civilization.

The young boys and girls who left Rhodesia to join the war either in Mozambique or Zambia came from all types of background: Christian or non-Christian homes, mission or government schools, as well as those who were unemployed. Several schools closed down because students had left to join the liberation movements. Consequently, as the parents understood more and more that it was a war of liberation, they did not want to be perceived to be opposed to the cause of liberation, let alone to be in opposition to their children. Indeed, the reason for these young people to join the war was clear: namely, to liberate their country, their parents, and themselves. Fear of death became secondary; the primary objective of joining the war was the liberation of the country. That message came through clearly each time these young people were brought to trial before the law courts of the land.

A number of new things started happening in the life of the Church. First, because the freedom of movement was restricted in the country, it was only the very dedicated ones who continued going to church. Also it meant the Church went underground, especially in the communal land. Some congregations stopped attending Sunday worship services altogether during that period. Often people met in their homes in small numbers. Second, the church began to sing a new song. They had a new song to sing and a new prayer to pray because things were no longer the same as before. Wives saw their husbands shot right before their eyes, while men saw their wives beaten up and even forced to prepare meals for the security forces. How could parents live in comfort or sleep in peace without their sons and daughters at home? How could a wife feel safe if her husband was taken away from her at midnight and "disappeared," never to be heard of again? Such was the kind of life people, especially those in the communal land, lived day in, day out. The young people in the struggle for liberation never forgot what they had been taught at home, and about the history of their people, especially those heroes like Chief Chingaira Makoni, Sekuru Kaguvi, Mbuya Nehanda, and many others. In that time of struggle, they learned to sing new songs about their struggle for liberation, their vulnerability, their courage, their heroes Sekuru Kaguvi and Mbuya Nehanda, the religion of their ancestors, and even about God, invoking His protection.

The musical artists in Rhodesia like Mapfumo, Mutukudzi, and many others responded by singing war songs. Indeed, the songs and prayers which were sung and heard in most churches throughout the land had likewise changed during that period. As a result, church worship brought parents and their children closer together once more in spirit, although they were many miles apart.

Between 1972 and 1980 the Church in Rhodesia, as an ecumenical body of the Christian Council of Rhodesia, responded to the war situation in a number of ways:

(1) Because of the Rhodesia Front government policies of separate development, increasingly the Christian Council came up with scholarships to enable large numbers of students to enroll at the local university who otherwise would not have had the opportunity. In 1975, for example, the Rhodesia Christian Council sponsored seventy-three students at the University of Rhodesia. Later on, scholarships were extended to those who had finished secondary school and were attending colleges of education, preparing to become teachers.

(2) The number of detainees in prisons increased with each passing day. Further, families would spend days, weeks, or months not knowing the whereabouts of one of their members who might have been detained. Several disappeared permanently in that manner. Therefore, the Rhodesia Christian Council utilized the facilities of the Legal Aid Committee, which had funds from people concerned about the deteriorating system of justice in the country, and assisted in defending many people brought before the courts or the bush courts that had been instituted. Often, the Legal Aid Committee was the only way to track persons taken away by the powers-that-be. I am fully aware of the problems the Legal Aid Committee faced in such investigations for I was a member of the executive committee of the Rhodesia Christian Council during that time. Countless individuals vanished without trace.

Further, the Christian Care Organization assisted many people, especially in the communal land, who had no shelter, food, clothes, or money to keep children in school (where schools were still operating). Also there were detainees in prison who needed to pursue private studies but had no financial means to do so. Their families at home also needed attention for many of the wives encountered financial problems with their husbands locked up, some for several years.

(3) The Catholic Commission for Justice and Peace did a magnificent job in educating the public about a number of atrocities that were committed by white security forces all over the country. In 1976, they published a booklet, *Civil War in Rhodesia*, that was very informative of the state of affairs in different parts of the country. Not only did the commission give a very detailed account of how various individuals were tortured or killed; photographs of several of those individuals were provided in the book.

The United Methodist Church

We have already said that while individual members of The United Methodist Church were free to join political parties of their own choice, United Methodists as a church never officially aligned themselves with one political view or party. Indeed they supported nationalism in a broad sense. It was in that spirit that even the episcopal leader of The United Methodist Church, Bishop Abel T. Muzorewa, in 1971 established the United African National Council (UANC) in order to oppose the proposals of the commission led by Lord Pearce. The mission was effectively accomplished and everybody was quite pleased with the results. United Methodists in particular were proud of their episcopal leader.

In 1977 Bishop Muzorewa and the UANC started serious negotiations with Prime Minister Ian Smith which led to an ill-fated "internal settlement." Whether the signing of the agreement for the so-called transitional government by four leaders inside the country, ignoring the strength of the liberation movements, was the right decision or a political blunder, history will tell. From that time on, it appeared the war raged between black leaders inside the country and those outside. Again, what was not understood then was that parents would always stand with their children in times of crisis. The merciless killing of about two thousand ZANLA guerrillas at Chimoi in 1977 by the Rhodesian forces drove parents closer to their children than ever before. The crisis was resolved only after talks among the leaders of ZANU, ZAPU, and the UANC in 1979 led to new elections in 1980, as a result of which Zimbabwe achieved an internationally recognized independence.

Between 1973 and 1977 the Annual Conference of The United Methodist Church in Rhodesia, as before, through its committee on Christian Social Concerns continued making strong pronouncements on issues that affected the Rhodesian society. The Annual Conference can be commended for its awareness of several social and political issues that affected the country during the 1970s. At the same time, the Annual Conference had courage to denounce what it believed was evil, and applauded that which it thought was right. This was in line with Methodist tradition concerning the Church's involvement in social issues. It may be that some United Methodists' sincere but excessive efforts to render ecclesiastical support to their bishop ended in their confusion of it with partisan political support. The failure to make that distinction might have created problems in The United Methodist Church, yet this might have been expected, for there are always enthusiasts among us.

The most positive thing about it all was that during the entire time the war was raging, The United Methodist Church, like every other church in the country, realized that the Church was a fellowship of the Holy Spirit called into existence by God through Christ. The Church was continuously strengthened by the Word of God and remained in prayer, always ready to take God's guidance during such difficult times. Indeed, though countless church buildings in the communal land had been either abandoned or destroyed by war and no one would dare ring church bells for fear of political recrimination, nevertheless Christians met in their homes secretly to pray for their children and for the war to come to an end.

When the Lancaster House Conference was convened in London on 10 September 1979, one could have said the resultant Zimbabwean independence was not due to the work of politicians and the liberation movements alone; the Church was also involved. The Church fed, clothed, and gave shelter to the freedom fighters, and it prayed for genuine settlement and political independence to come to a new Rhodesia.

As numerous political parties, which had mushroomed in the 1970s, crumpled with the dawn of independent Zimbabwe, the Church of Christ emerged from the ashes of war stronger, wiser, and more dedicated and daring to move forward than ever before.

Summary

(1) The war of liberation was a direct result of colonial usurpation of land from the African people including a harsh and hostile rule imposed by colonialists on the African people.

(2) Several attempts were made in 1966, 1968, 1971, and 1976 to avert the war by peacefully resolving the Rhodesian crisis, but with no success until 1979.

(3) Almost all churches in Zimbabwe supported the cause of the war of liberation; this accounts for their direct support and that given indirectly through other agents by offering their moral and material support to the freedom fighters.

Chapter 12

The Church in a New Nation

On 18 April 1980, Zimbabwe's Independence Day, the Honorable Prime Minister Robert Gabriel Mugabe in his message invited the new nation to a mood and spirit of reconciliation:

> As we become a new people, we are called to be constructive, progressive and forever forward looking, for we cannot afford to be men of yesterday. . . .
>
> Our new nation requires every one of us to be a new man with a new mind, a new heart and a new spirit that must unite and not divide. This is the human essence that must form the core of our political change and national independence. If yesterday I fought you as an enemy, today you have become a friend and ally with the same national interest.

The message of Prime Minister Mugabe could not have been strange to Christians or to the citizens of Zimbabwe. For a people who had gone through a bitter war for over a decade, a war that had divided the nation, institutions, families, and even churches, the call to national unity came as the most profound and healing message of all.

The call to national reconciliation also went to the churches, preparing all Zimbabwean Christians to face new challenges and opportunities which Independence was to present to the Church in relation to God's mission for the sake of abundant life for all God's people. So this chapter will examine how the churches in Zimbabwe adapted or should have adapted themselves to the new life of independent Zimbabwe. Four areas of concern stand out prominently for our examination: the reality of the African situation, evangelization in Africa, Africanization of the faith, and church participation in the nation-building program.

The Reality of the African Situation

First, the Church of Christ must be able to distinguish the content of faith from culture. About thirty years ago, a missionary from overseas tried to assist an African congregation in Zimbabwe (then Rhodesia) to look more Christian by suggesting that they sit as couples in church worship services. Most of the congregations, especially those in villages, to this day prefer to have men sit on one side of the church and women on the other. But that missionary even went on to say that it was part of the Christian faith for husbands and wives to sit together in worship. To his surprise, the church lost almost all the men the following Sunday, for they chose to stay away from church worship rather than yield to the new seating arrangement, which, in light of traditional Shona culture, struck them as awkward.

As both a theological and sociological institution, every church needs constantly to examine its need for liberation in order to be an effective agent for the liberating message. It needs liberation from innumerable foreign models to understand Christianity in Africa today; it must be able to distinguish faith from mere culture. Indeed, Christians in Africa have been called everything under the sun. Apart from their denominational names, they have been called evangelicals, ecumenicals, sectarians, liberals, conservatives, and much else besides. Most of these terms or labels are imported from elsewhere and do not accurately convey the same meaning in the African context. Such models of interpreting Christianity have aroused not only the scandal of the disunity of the Church but have also posed a potential danger to the political unity of the peoples of Africa. All this points to the importance of the Church in Africa indicating that it needs liberating itself. A liberated church derives its identity from Christ as well as from mission in its contextual situation. Such a church will reflect upon the fact of Christ in its midst in the context of the issues and struggles characteristic of the everyday human situation.

Before Independence in Zimbabwe, all kinds of myths were spread by successive governments and by some in the church hierarchy. It was believed that the white minority in the country was defending Western Christian civilization and that they were fighting a holy war against communism. The argument continued in some quarters until the collapse of communism in Eastern Europe in the late 1980s. It has now obviously become clearer to most people that the struggle by such a minority was really to maintain their privileged position and to sustain a political and economic system that exploited the majority of Zimbabweans. At the same time, Zimbabwean churches seemed to be satisfied with an imported theology passed on to them as denominational heritage. It was not until the struggle escalated to involve armed liberation movements that churches in Zimbabwe began serious theological reflection. The liberation movements attracted the children, not only those who came from non-Christian backgrounds, but also those young boys and girls from mission centers and Christian families. Hence the question: Should Christians be involved in violence in order to attain their desired goals after all nonviolent approaches have failed? That was a merely academic question for people who were not involved in the war, for those who did not have children involved in the struggle; yet it was quite the contrary for Christian communities who read the Bible out of a violent situation.

With the increase in reports of hangings and brutal interrogations, with rewards being offered to those who volunteered information pertaining to liberation movements, people in Rhodesia learned to ask the right questions: Is it not our children who are involved in the armed struggle? Why did they leave our homes and schools? Why have they chosen the armed struggle approach? Such questions had an existential authenticity. It was not time for imported answers. Indeed, it was better to have no answers than to accept answers that were irrelevant. The result was that not only the churches but the entire population was drawn into the struggle for the liberation of their own country. It was the liberation struggle of a new people, the Zimbabweans.

The churches realized it was not the time for canned answers and they grieved with the rest of the people. Above all they groaned inwardly as they waited for real solutions to a complex situation. Such groaning and deep sighing have been best expressed in the new African hymns which Christian communities began singing. Once the children left homes and schools for the war of liberation, the singing in churches could not remain the same: How could they sing a foreign song with a daughter or son in the bush? How could they pray sincerely a prayer that had no relevance to their fate and that of their children?

It was one of the most crucial times in the history of the Church in Rhodesia. The Church had to rediscover for itself its identity around Christ. It became conscious of the need for new theological reflection and expression of its faith. Now the Church in Zimbabwe has a vital experience to share with the rest of Christendom. In their own particular locality, churches attained a sense of the universality of the Church when they learned of the experiences of the churches in Angola, Mozambique, Kenya, and many other countries which had also suffered for their liberation.

Second, it is essential for the church to cultivate healthy working relationships with the state for the purpose of God's mission. During colonial days white missionaries and the churches they founded in Rhodesia often enjoyed protection from the colonial flag. Even if the missionaries did not come from the same colonial power that then ruled Rhodesia, they felt sympathetic to one another because they shared a common European cultural background. It was only natural that such a feeling of togetherness had to exist.

The Church in Zimbabwe needs to realize that the revolution that has brought about Independence calls for new structures and relationships with society. The Church cannot expect the old relationships and structures of colonial days to sustain them after an independent government has come into existence. Furthermore, loyalties need to change. A church in Zimbabwe that continues to perceive its life and mission only in light of expatriates today has not taken the Zimbabwean reality seriously; neither has it taken itself seriously enough as the community of Christ.

A third issue, one that the Church in Zimbabwe should be ashamed of, is that of excessive denominationalism or sectarianism. African governments detest this phenomenon. There have been situations in other communities where the multiplicity of independent churches has been considered a threat to national unity. By the same token one cannot overlook the fact that multiplicity of denominations tends to create political tensions, and subsequently poses an equally threatening situation to national unity. Some church groups have come to Africa with good intentions of spreading the Good News of the Kingdom of God by translating the Bible. Yet, when some of these groups become overly enthusiastic and try to translate the Bible into the language of every ethnic group in Africa, this fosters every small group and slows down the process of cultural and political unification of the people and standardization of languages.

At a time when several governments in Africa are struggling for national unity and peace for the benefit of all God's people, the

Church in Africa needs to take the issues of national unity and nation building seriously. When the Church becomes a divisive factor to national unity, the Church should take time to discern what its mission is supposed to be for the sake of all God's people. Narrow mindedness in some programs needs to be replaced with supportive efforts by the Church to help liberate the peoples of Africa.

Evangelization in Africa

Evangelization is that process in the life of the community around Christ where the Christian faith becomes good news to a people and incarnate in their cultural life. One may talk about the "inculturation" of the faith, but the theological basis is the good news of Christ Jesus who became man (Phil. 2:5; John 1:14) and through whom all people are reconciled to God (Cor. 5:18, 19). The time has come for the proclamation of our witness to the gospel (John 15:27) and reflection upon the Christian faith to be presented in cultural thought-forms and imagery that are relevant and meaningful to the people of Africa. Such a task of evangelization does not necessarily mean accommodating or manipulating the Christian faith in cultural ways people might choose. The relationship of the gospel to culture is more dialectical and dynamic than complementary. It is not always a comfortable relationship.

While evangelization is an ongoing process of disseminating the Christian faith, each generation of Christians is charged with the responsibility to the task in their own particular situation. Thus evangelism becomes a conscious effort and function of the Church to witness to that which God is doing through Christ (2 Cor. 5:18) and to participate fully in God's mission as "ambassadors for Christ" (2 Cor. 5:20).

In Zimbabwe and the rest of Africa, far from meaning a specialized activity performed once or twice a year and for only some people in the congregation, evangelism has come to mean nothing less than the whole process of sharing the Christian faith by the whole Christian community. All are involved: clergy and laity, men and women, old and young, full members of the church and those still on probation—all must be involved in the task of evangelism. The credentials necessary to the task are simply belonging to a

Christian community. At the symposium on "The Bible and Evangelization" in Nairobi, the churches understood evangelization as

> a dynamic means of transmitting the words of God to all men. It means witnessing for Christ by the whole Christian community through proclamation, service and fellowship.[1]

The Africa Task Force, which included eight African United Methodist Annual Conferences, defined evangelism as the ministry of the whole Church. Even during times of national political struggle when churches are forced to go underground, their witness to the reality of Christ demonstrates the genuine Christian understanding of victory through the cross and hope in Christ Jesus. Even in time of agony and suffering, many identify with Christ and confess Him as their only hope.

The Churches of Africa are growing rapidly as they respond with new forms of evangelism to meet the needs of the people. While some are still adaptations of Western models, others have emerged out of distinctly African cultural roots. For example, United Methodists in Africa note that in Zaire traditional evangelism and mass evangelism were still effective. In Liberia "The Godpower Movement" was a vibrant source of renewal and evangelistic outreach within the Church in the 1970s. In Angola in the 1970s Bishop Emilio de Carvalho of The United Methodist Church pointed out that

> one can witness a tremendous awakening and revival . . . both in rural and urban areas. The class leaders, local preachers and volunteer workers are necessary and effective 'touchstones' for evangelism.

There are four ways in which some African churches including Zimbabwe seem to thrive in their evangelization. First, evangelization takes place within the Christian community itself. In Zimbabwe there is a traditional village practice where men sit outdoors around the village fire after a day's work. Boys between the ages of ten and eighteen are expected to bring firewood to this place called *dare*. The *dare* is a very important institution in the life of a traditional village. In spite of the informality, it remains highly significant, especially to the young people. A number of activities go on, such as entertainment in the form of folktales, riddles, and proverbs; and instruction of the young people in the skills they should have in order to earn their livelihood: cultivating the land, blacksmithing, hunting, fishing, and many others. This is the place where the boys are taught the facts of life and the expectations of a good family life. However, the *dare* is primarily a place for men. No woman is expected at the *dare* unless the headman has called for a special *dare* for purposes of trial. Girls have a place of their own. Usually they meet indoors after they have finished their household duties.

The most important person at the *dare* is an elderly man, recognized for his wise counseling and traditional instruction of the young people. One could say everything revolves around him at the *dare*. In a similar vein, the elderly woman around whom the girls gather, offers instruction to enable them to take their places effectively in community life and society at large.

The solidarity of Christians around Christ is derived from the centrality of Christ amidst his community. As in the *dare*, Christ is the wise leader and counselor around whom life and all activities of the community find meaning and direction. He is the giver of life, the healer of the sick. Yet unlike the African traditional *dare*, the community around Christ has no gender divisions, for all are equal in the sight of God.

Some of the independent churches in Zimbabwe have come to realize the importance of and the centrality of community life in the fellowship of the Holy Spirit. To attend meetings and celebrations in such communities means hearing, seeing, feeling the gospel; that is, witnessing the cutting edge of evangelization in the context of a Christian community where the love of God for all persons is demonstrated by deeds of concern and caring for one another (Matt. 25:35-36; Acts 2:44-47) and bearing one another's burdens (Gal. 6:2).

This is what is meant by incarnational evangelism: an evangelism whose message is capable of penetrating into the heart of the cultural life of every people in order to conscientize men and women about this newness of life (2 Cor. 5:17) and to awaken them "into a living hope through the resurrection of Jesus Christ" (1 Peter 1:3). It is an evangelism that seeks to relate this central message of God in Christ to every culture for purposes of effective communication of the gospel, while culture is at the same time subjected to judgment by the same gospel. The greatest thrust of such an evangelism comes always in a communal context where the gospel witnessed in the power of the Holy Spirit is like "the yeast that a woman took and mixed in with three measures of flour until all of it was leavened" (Matt. 13:33).

Second, evangelism takes place in the extended congregations. In Zimbabwe most congregations are flexible, if not fluid. They can easily visit one another as congregations. They have adopted the practice that stems from rural African life where people like to do things together, just as people would help one another in their fields or in raising a house together. During the weekend, two or more local congregations come together and spend the nights singing, giving testimonies, preaching, and praying together.

A quick glance at the continent-wide evangelization of Africa, from 1918 to the 1930s, shows that in countries like Ethiopia, Uganda, Mozambique, and Zimbabwe the task of evangelization was carried out by lay people. Today a similar approach to evangelization is used by several independent churches: the Kimbanguist Church in Zaire, the Church of Nicholas B. H. Bhengu of South Africa, the Apostolic Church of Johane Marange of Zimbabwe and probably many others. It is interesting that such gatherings are crossing denominational lines, and even including Roman Catholics. Furthermore, the clergy do not have to be there; if they are, their role is exhortation and not preaching. The latter is lay people's responsibility. Not only has this approach created a spirit of community and ecumenicity in the life of the Church, this is also where evangelization is taking place.

Third, evangelism takes place through small groups. A pastor in Zimbabwe shared a conversation with his colleagues about a woman who had left her church (one of a mainstream denomination) to join an independent one. On being asked why she had left, the woman replied that she had a problem. After living with her husband for many years, she still had borne no child. After attending her new church, she reported that she had joined a group of women who were very conscious of her problem and came to pray with her many times (Gal. 6:2). These women believed that joining together in the spirit of prayer could bring comfort, hope, and victory even if she did not have the child she wanted. Not only do new converts come from other churches; even more so, they come from outside the Christian communities.

These small groups have taken different forms and emphasize different aspect of their task. They have emphasized prayer, Bible study, and sharing of experiences. At times they have become known as house churches and prayer groups. In small Christian groups with a family atmosphere and spirit, no one believer fights against evil forces and temptations alone; such fellowship enables Christian growth and character. These small groups understand themselves as tributaries to the main fellowship; that is, to the local church or parish. The author has noticed that a number of mainstream churches and almost all independent churches have given freedom to their members for this kind of evangelization. Often new members have come to church through such groups of fellowship.

Africanization of the Faith

Africanization is the way the Church in Africa relates the Christian faith to the African situation. It is the affirmation that the God of the ancestors, who has been acknowledged throughout the continent, has now come to his people through Christ Jesus, His Son. It is also the affirmation of the historical reality of the African cultural context which shapes the African voice to answer the call of Christ. In other words, Africanization of the Christian faith is a crucial factor in the proclamation of the gospel in Africa. It means a new appreciation of African culture and religion. It involves organizational and leadership styles which emphasize African spirituality and authenticity in human relations. It involves worship in which church architecture, music, liturgy, and art are authentic expressions of the African religious experience. It means using African images and idioms in preaching Christ. Africanization means contextualization of the Christian faith for Africa.

Allow me to cite some examples of Africanization which the Church in Zimbabwe has experienced. For many years the music in Zimbabwe was dominated by foreign cultures. Secular music which boomed from radio and television was mainly Western. Worship music on Sunday was similarly a transplanting of denominational hymns from the West. This is an experience which many churches in Zimbabwe have had at one time or another. With the coming of the struggle for liberation, especially in the 1970s, the picture has been changing. The churches have shown increasing interest in what we would call "typical" African music, accompanied by African instruments. Enthusiasm for indigenous music has been evident as much among adults and youths as in ecumenical gatherings. Churches have been wise to encourage this growing

171

phenomenon. In Zimbabwe, churches have sponsored music work-
shops for ecumenical gatherings, especially where the youth are
involved.

What is even more interesting in this respect, however, is that
the war in Zimbabwe gave rise to Zimbabwean indigenous music
that genuinely portrays the peoples' philosophical and religious
view. Because the traditional African world embraces everything
under the religious cover, songs about the liberation struggle have
helped to conscientize the people of Zimbabwe with regard to
understanding who they are and where their cultural resources for
support and sustenance lie. Such war-tempered songs reveal not
only the atrocious results of the war, they also include an appeal
to the ancestors and to God. They identify the struggle for liberation
with mission and a sense of responsibility; this is a struggle for all
people that demands a sense of dedication. Music such as this has
effectively conscientized the whole nation in the space of a short
time. This is Africanization at its best. What a source of materials
for understanding people and who they really are before God!

A second set of examples comes from what I have used personally in an attempt to interpret the Christian faith by using ordinary
Zimbabwean African customs and cultural practices. First, among
the Shona people of Zimbabwe there is a custom called *kubombera*
(taking refuge with somebody). This means that if a child has done
something wrong and a parent takes a stick to hit the child, the
child can run to somebody for refuge. The best person to serve as
refuge is an aunt or grandmother. As the child runs to the aunt or
the grandmother and takes refuge behind the back of either of these
adults, the child will say "*ndabombera!*" Adults practice the custom too in situations in which they need protection. For example,
a woman terrorized by her husband can seek refuge. When one
claims to *bombera* behind somebody, he or she should not be
touched. If one hits a child, one's own or another's, who has
bombera behind someone, it would be an offense serious enough
to be settled by the elders in the village, for one will not have
honored the individual with whom the victim took refuge.

This is what Paul means when he writes to the Christians in
Corinth: "God was in Christ reconciling the world to himself, not
counting their trespasses against them, and entrusting to us the
message of reconciliation" (2 Cor. 5:19). In our African context this
means that in Christ Jesus, God has provided an aunt or grand-

mother for the sinner to *bombera*; God has chosen to reconcile his people to himself through Christ. It is God who has moved out and has led us to meet him in Christ. In addition, in our aunt or grandmother (Christ Jesus), God has found "a way in which his love for the sinner and his wrath against sin can be accommodated . . . and justify the man—the sinful man who relies on faith in Jesus." As a child *bombera* behind someone in order for his case to have a fair hearing, so does a man stand justified before God in Christ Jesus.

Second, in a number of African countries mothers carry their babies on their backs. In Zimbabwe, they use a specially tailored cloth called *mbereko* to keep the child warm and in a comfortable position. Many mothers have to hold and play with other mothers' babies when they enter a house where other women are present; they happily share in the holding of the babies.

When a mother is asked by another to hold her baby, the mother brings down the baby from her back in the *mbereko* and hands it over to her. Upon receiving the baby, the recipient re-arranges the baby to make sure it is comfortable. If the weather is warm, the recipient strips the *mbereko* off. If the baby needs more warmth, the *mbereko* is wrapped more closely. Above all, the baby must be comfortable on the lap of the recipient for both to enjoy each other. It follows that for the transmission of the Christian faith to be the good news to other people it must be a continuous process of Incarnation. The gospel—like a baby going from the hands of one mother to another—remains the same (Heb. 13:8), but for it to become the good news, the recipient's cultural thought-forms and patterns of thinking and expression have to play an active role.

The adaptation of African understanding and interpretation of the Christian faith which affirms the living realities of the African context is Africanization of the faith. This process inevitably begins as the Christian faith is communicated to a new people. The dynamism and vitality of the African Church is indebted to innumerable Christian communities that have discovered this secret as the true meaning of the experience of Pentecost when people hear the gospel in thought-forms which make sense to them (Acts 2:8).

Church Participation in Nation-Building Programs

The concept of nation building is firmly imbedded in some books of the Bible. For example the book of Nehemiah teaches us about Nehemiah and how he left his employment as a cupbearer to the Persian King in order to go and rebuild Jerusalem. It was upon receiving the message about the destruction of Jerusalem after its citizens had been taken into captivity in Persia—especially the message about how the city had been left in ruins with walls destroyed, gates burned down, and about how all who had escaped into the desert were in great misery and in danger of death by starvation—that Israel as a people understood themselves as the chosen ones who were in danger of losing their faith in Jehovah and thus left Nehemiah to weep. Consequently, Nehemiah decided to go back to Jerusalem to rebuild the city of his fathers so that his people would not suffer disgrace.

From its beginning, the Church in Zimbabwe has been involved in nation building. It has been part and parcel of the church's task of evangelization. As a matter of fact, the Church in Zimbabwe was a loner in establishing schools and clinics in the rural areas. This was also true when it came to teaching people rudimentary skills in modern agriculture, carpentry, and construction of better houses. To this day, one is not surprised to find that a fairly high percentage of persons who hold high national positions in Zimbabwe came up through the Church.

Realizing that numerous church buildings, school buildings, and clinics in the rural areas had been either destroyed or had deteriorated because they had not been used during the war period, with the advent of Independence, churches worked jointly with the government on a program of reconstruction. The Zimbabwe Council of Churches played a significant role in coordinating churches' activities. Joint reconstruction programs were initiated with the cooperation and participation of ecumenical partners based overseas, the Zimbabwe Government and the ecumenical community in Zimbabwe. With the program of resettling people throughout the country by the government, churches sensitive to the task of mission found new opportunities in reaching people either by meeting their immediate and basic needs in providing food, shelter, and water or by starting new congregations in the new resettlement areas; for others it was both. The Zimbabwe Council of Churches list of its priority projects for 1986–87 is a good example of the church's participation in the program of nation building. Churches planned involvement in the following areas: education, water development, food production, health care, vocational training, and other community services. Indeed, churches in Zimbabwe have realized their unity in Christ through participation in the mission to resettle people who for years had been slaves in their own land. Furthermore, churches have gone into partnership with the government and assist in raising the living standards for citizens of Zimbabwe.

All this points to our holistic understanding of the gospel in Africa which views life around Christ in its totality of human relationships. Consequently, the tendency is not to segment life into separate spheres with the implied individualism and the tendency to want to polarize relationships; i.e. the vertical against the horizontal, the personal against the social, and the conservative against the liberal. African Christians who may spend the whole evening in a church prayer meeting are the same people who periodically march in political rallies for their total liberation. For them religion does not signal divorce from social involvement, for both belong together. Such an orientation is derived from the African traditional religious life; happily such an orientation finds harmony with biblical teaching.

Such a holistic understanding of the gospel is clearly expressed in "The Confession of Alexandria" formulated by the General Committee of the All-Africa Conference of Churches when they met in Egypt in 1976:

> Our commitment to the struggle for human liberation is one of the ways we confess our faith in an incarnate God, who loved us so much that he came among us in our own human form, suffered, was crucified for our redemption and was raised for our justification. Such undeserved grace evokes a response of joy that we are seeking to express and to share in language, modes of spirituality, liturgical forms, patterns of mission and structures of organization that belong uniquely to our own cultural context.[2]

Therefore, it means we are talking about witnessing to the holistic gospel and we anticipate healing or liberation wherever there is hurt, depending upon our historical circumstances. Healing that occurs in one aspect of life is healing for the wholeness of life. And no single aspect of life should be neglected at the expense of the other, for to do so is to neglect wholeness. How correct Paul was when he wrote to the Corinthians about the wholeness or oneness of the Church: "If one member suffers, all suffer together with it" (1 Cor. 12:26). It means suffering inflicted on the social life

175

of a people affects the spiritual and the physical aspects of the whole body as well.

As churches tailor their lives according to their experiences both in Zimbabwe and in Africa as a whole, they have increasingly been attracted by this holistic understanding of the gospel. The purpose of the holistic gospel of the Kingdom is to bring healing and salvation to the whole person (John 13:10), to the whole family (Luke 19:92; Acts 16:33), to the whole nation (Rev. 21:24), and to the whole of creation (Rom. 8:18-24). For African people today, healing brings liberation which touches multiple dimensions of human life; that is, the political, economic, socio-cultural, and religious—all embraced together as the spiritual dimensions of life.

Summary

(1) With the advent of Independence in the country, churches had to re-identify themselves as well as redefining their mission goals.

(2) Evangelization remained the central task of the church and was understood and carried out using models that were relevant to the African churches.

(3) Africanization of the Christian faith is an inevitable process of accommodating the faith.

(4) Finally, the African churches are engaged in the process of nation building especially in the area of leadership training.

Appendix 1

Timeline of Events

A Brief Chronology of Key Events Relating to
the History of The United Methodist Church
in Zimbabwe

1889 — Cecil Rhodes forms the British South Africa Company under charter from Great Britain; white settlement begins
1897 — Bishop Hartzell first visits Zimbabwe
1898 — Opening of Old Mutare Mission on land granted by British South Africa Company
1901 — Establishment of the East Central Africa Mission Conference
1905 — Opening of Mutambara Mission
1909 — Opening of Murewa Mission
1911 — Opening of Mutoko Mission
1916 — Establishment of the Rhodesia Mission Conference
1918 — Revival begins at first camp meeting in Old Mutare
1918 — Origin of Vabvuwi veMethodist Episcopal Church (Methodist Episcopal Church Men)
1919 — Training School founded at Old Mutare
1921 — David Mandisodza is first African to be ordained as Deacon
1922 — Opening of Nyadiri Mission
1923 — Southern Rhodesia becomes self-governing Crown Colony
1927 — Establishment of the Board of Home Missions and Church Extension
1928 — Establishment of the African Christian Convention
1929 — Clifford Faku, David Mandisodza, Thomas Marange, and Reginald Ngonyama are first Africans to be ordained as Elders

1929 — Origin of Rukwadzano rweVadzimai veMethodist Episcopal Church (Women's Society of Christian Service of the Methodist Episcopal Church)

1931 — Establishment of the Rhodesia Annual Conference

1931 — Land Apportionment Act establishes apartheid, legally separating white and black lands

1932 — Schism of Johane Marange

1938 — Establishment of Ngariende (The Africa Missionary Society)

1939 — The Methodist Episcopal Church becomes The Methodist Church

1957 — Organization of African National Congress (ANC) of Southern Rhodesia

1960 — Organization of the Zimbabwe Christian Council

1961 — Organization of Zimbabwe African People's Union (ZAPU)

1963 — Organization of Zimbabwe African National Union (ZANU)

1965 — "Unilateral Declaration of Independence" by the (white) Rhodesian government

1966 — Battle of Chinhoyi begins War of Independence, which continues and intensifies through the late 1960s and 1970s

1967 — Establishment of the Urban Program of the Christian Council of Rhodesia

1968 — The Methodist Church becomes The United Methodist Church

1968 — First (ecumenical) Rhodesian Urban Consultation

1969 — Land Tenure Act reinforces apartheid

1971 — Organization of the United African National Council (UANC)

1980 — Zimbabwe achieves independence on 18 April; Robert Mugabe becomes first Prime Minister

1980 — Establishment of the Zimbabwe Annual Conference

1992 — Founding of Africa University

1997 — Centennial of Methodism in Zimbabwe

Appendix 2

List of Bishops

Bishops Who Served
the Zimbabwe Annual Conference
and its Predecessor Conferences of
The United Methodist Church
in Zimbabwe

William Taylor (1884–1896)

Joseph C. Hartzell (1896–1916)

Eben S. Johnson (1917–1936)

John M. Springer (1936–1944)

Nowell S. Booth (1944–1956)

Ralph E. Dodge (1956–1968)

Abel T. Muzorewa (1968–1985)

James K. Mathews (1985–1986)

Abel T. Muzorewa (1986–1992)

Christopher Jokomo (1992–present)

Abbreviations

MECAMC = *Minutes of the East Central Africa Mission Conference* (1901– 1915).

MRMC = *Minutes of the Rhodesia Mission Conference* (1916–1930).

JRAC = *Journal of the Rhodesia Annual Conference* (1931–1980).

JZAC = *Journal of the Zimbabwe Annual Conference* (1980–1996).

Notes

Notes to Preface

1. *MECAMC* (1901), 6.
2. Ibid., viii.
3. Kuedu Dadzi, "Africa: One Continent, Two Faces," *Black Business Digest* (July 1972): 34.
4. Eugen Rosenstock-Hussey, *Out of Revolution: Autobiography of Western Man* (Norwich, CT: Arge Books, 1969), 524.
5. Jürgen Moltmann, *Theology of Hope* (New York: Harper and Row, 1967), 20.
6. Basil Davidson, *A Guide to African History*, 2nd ed. (New York: Doubleday and Company, Inc., 1971), 99–100.

Notes to Chapter 1

1. T. A. Beetham, *Christianity and the New Africa* (London: Pall Mall Press, 1967), 10.
2. "History of the United Methodist Church," *Umbowo* 55, no. 12 (December 1972): 3.
3. William Taylor, *Story of My Life* (New York: Hunt & Eaton, 1896), 691.
4. *The African News* 1, no. 5 (May 1889): 175.
5. *MECAMC* (1901), 21.
6. Ibid.

7. *The Book of Discipline of The United Methodist Church* (Africa Central Conference Edition, 1990), 4.

8. Joseph C. Hartzell, *The Africa Mission of the Episcopal Church* (February 1909), 46.

9. Ibid.

10. *MECAMC* (1913), 7.

11. "History of the United Methodist Church," *Umbowo* (October 1972): 3.

12. *MECAMC* (1913), 7.

13. Ibid. (1901), viii.

14. Ibid., vii.

15. Henry I. James, *Missions in Rhodesia Under The Methodist Episcopal Church* (Old Mutare: Rhodesia Press, 1935), viii.

Notes to Chapter 2

1. *MECAMC* (1905), 28.

2. Ibid. (1907), 42.

3. T. O. Ranger, *State and Church in Southern Rhodesia, 1919–1939* (Salisbury: The Central Africa Historical Association, 1958), 7.

Notes to Chapter 3

1. *MECAMC* (1907), 32.

2. Ibid. (1912), 1.

3. Ibid. (1901), v.

4. William Taylor, *Story of My Life* (New York: Hunt and Eaton, 1986), 696.

5. *MECAMC* (1901), 25.

6. Ibid.

7. "What Christian Life Means," *The Missionary Review of the World* (May 1938): 242.

8. *MRMC* (1921), 27.

9. Ibid. (1923), 40.

10. *MECAMC* (1910), 69.

11. Ibid., 70.

12. *MRMC* (1916), 7.

13. *MECAMC* (1910), 50.

14. Ibid.

Notes to Chapter 4

1. *MECAMC* (1907), 24.

2. Ibid. (1909), 30.

3. Ibid. (1907), 27.

4. Ibid. (1908), 51.

5. Ibid.

6. Ibid., 41.
7. Ibid. (1905), 34.
8. Ibid., 35.

Notes to Chapter 5

1. Janson Machiwenyika, *History of the Manyika People*, trans. by W. S. Musewe in 1943 (an unpublished manuscript in MA 14/1/2, National Archives). Janson Machiwenyika was a teacher, and well known in the Conference of The Methodist Episcopal Church for being conversant with African customs and the history of the Manyika people. By the time of his death in 1924, he had accumulated hundreds of pages of history and folklore stories that he had written (*Journal of the Conference*, [1924], 35).
2. *MRMC* (1919), 42.
3. "The Mission Extension of The Methodist Church in Africa (1816–1896)," *Umbowo* (December 1972): 37.
4. Machiwenyika, 1.
5. *MRMC* (1919), 39.
6. Ibid. (1928), 35.
7. Ibid. (1917), 62.
8. Bengt G. M. Sundkler, *Bantu Prophets in South Africa*, 2nd ed. (London: Oxford University Press, 1961), 53.
9. Ibid.
10. *MRMC* (1919), 38.
11. Ibid. (1927), 33.

Notes to Chapter 6

1. "The All-Africa Seminar on the Christian Home and Family," *Family* 17 (April 10, 1963): 19.
2. *JRAC* (1942), 244.
3. Ibid., 243.
4. Ibid., 244.
5. Ibid. (1947), 29.
6. Beetham, 12.
7. *MRMC* (1919), 33–34.
8. S. E. M. Pheko, *Christianity Through African Eyes* (Lusaka: Daystar Publications Ltd., 1969), 5.

Notes to Chapter 7

1. "The Mission Extension of The United Methodist Church in Africa," *Umbowo* (October 1972): 5.
2. *JRAC* (1954), 271.
3. *Bhuku reRukwadzano rweVadzimai veUnited Methodist Church*

["The Book of Rules for the Women of The United Methodist Church"] (Umtali: Rhodesia Mission Press, 1969), 3.

4. Ibid., 23.

5. David Bosch, "The Question of the Mission of Today," *Journal of Theology for Southern Africa* (December 1972): 14.

6. "Scholars Debate Role of Corporations in Third World Economics," *The Christian Century* (29 November 1972): 121.

Notes to Chapter 8

1. Newell S. Booth, *The Cross Over Africa* (New York: Friendship Press, 1945), 2.

2. Stanlake Samkange, *African Saga* (Nashville: Abingdon Press, 1971), 173.

3. Ibid., 174.

4. Chancellor Williams, *The Destruction of Black Civilization* (Dubuque: Kendall/Hunt Publishing Company, 1971), 184.

5. James S. Spady, "The Ancient Zimbabwe Empire," *Negro History Bulletin* 34, no. 2 (February 1971): 184.

6. Samkange, *Saga*, 176.

7. Stanlake Samkange, *Origins of Rhodesia* (New York: Frederick A. Prager, 1968), 78.

8. Ibid., 77.

9. L. H. Gann, *A History of Southern Rhodesia* (New York: Humanities Press, 1969).

10. Rukudzo Murapa, "Osagyefo Pan Africanist Leader," *Black World* (July 1972): 20.

11. *Drumbeats from Kampala* (London: Lutherworth Press, 1963), 60.

12. Ibid., 60–61.

13. "Copy of a letter received in December from Guy Clutton-Clock, of the Cold Comfort Farm Society, Box 2097, Salisbury, Southern Rhodesia Ninth Newsletter," 1.

Notes to Chapter 9

1. *The Mission of the Church in Urban Africa*: (Report of the Consultation held in Nairobi, Kenya, March 1961), 26.

2. J. Clyde Mitchell, *An Outline of the Sociological Background to African Labour* (Ensign Publishers, Pvt. Ltd., 1961), 76 ff.

3. *MRMC* (1924), 40.

4. Mitchell, 83–84.

5. "Summary of Important Provision of the Land Tenure Act (1969)." This summary statement was prepared by a special committee of The United Methodist Church to help people understand the meaning of the Act.

6. "Harare Residents Criticise New Rents Exploitation," *Christian Mirror* (October 1970): 1.

7. *The Church's Mission in Rhodesia's Towns* (Report of the First Rhodesian Urban Church Consultation—Salisbury, 5–8 December 1958), 64.

8. "Rhodesia Address Given by Bishop Abel Tendekayi Muzorewa," (General Conference, Atlanta, Georgia, 22 April 1972), 5.

9. *The Mission of the Church in Urban Africa* (Report on the Consultation held in Nairobi, March 1961), 26.

10. *JRAC* (1973), 152.

11. Ibid. (1961), 83.

12. Ibid. (1962), 92.

13. Gibson Winter, *The New Creation as Metropolis*, 2nd ed. (New York: The Macmillan Company, 1966), 2–3.

14. *The Church's Mission in Rhodesia's Towns*, 7–8.

15. A. Adebgola, "The Church Freed and United for Mission," *Ministry* 2, no. 4. (July 1963): 168.

Notes to Chapter 10

1. *JRAC* (1970), 63.

2. David Bosch, "The Question of Mission Today," *Journal of Theology for Southern Africa* (December 1972): 14.

3. Ranger, *State and Church in Southern Rhodesia* (1919–39), 23.

4. Ibid., 6.

5. Ibid., 10.

6. L. H. Gann, *A History of Southern Africa* (New York: Humanities Press, 1969), 258–59.

7. Ibid.

8. *JRAC* (1968), 79.

9. Ibid. (1969), 88.

10. Ibid. (1977), 92.

11. *MRMC* (1917), 26.

12. *JRAC* (1972), 85–96.

13. R. T. Parsons and R. N. C. Nwosu, *Christian Ministry—Vital Issues* (Ibadan: Abiodun Printing Works, 1965), 39–40.

14. *JRAC* (1956), 95.

Notes to Chapter 11

1. Gann, *History of Southern Africa*, 136.

2. Maurice Nyagumbo, *With the People* (Salisbury: Mardon Printers [Pvt] Ltd., 1980), 193.

3. Robert G. Mugabe, *Our War of Liberation* (Gweru: Mambo Press, 1983), 3.

4. Ken Flower, *Serving Secretly* (London: John Murray Publishers, Ltd., 1987), 114.

5. Ibid., 119.
6. Ibid., 151.
7. Ibid., 191–93.
8. Ibid., 214.
9. *A New People, A New Church* (Hertogenbosch, Holland: Dutch Missionary Council, 1980), 96.
10. Ibid.

Notes to Chapter 12

1. *New World Outlook* (November 1978): 8.
2. "The Confession of Alexandria" (General Committee of the All-Africa Conference of Churches, 1976).

Select Bibliography

Primary Sources

Minutes of the East Central Africa Mission Conference (1901–1915).
Minutes of the Rhodesia Mission Conference (1916–1930).
Journal of the Rhodesia Annual Conference (1931–1979).
Journal of the Zimbabwe Annual Conference (1980–1996).

Secondary Sources

Adebgola, A. "The Church Freed and United for Mission." *Ministry* 2, no. 4. (July 1963).

The African News, vol. 1, no. 5 (May 1889).

"The All-Africa Seminar on the Christian Home and Family." *Family* 17 (10 April 1963).

Beetham, T. A. *Christianity and the New Africa*. London: Pall Mall Press, 1967.

Bhuku reRukwadzano rweVadzimai veUnited Methodist Church ["The Book of Rules for the Women of The United Methodist Church"]. Umtali: Rhodesia Mission Press, 1969.

Bloy, Philip, ed. *Papers on Urban-Industrial Issues in Africa and the Challenge for the Church*. Somerset: Variprint, 1970.

Booth, Newell S. *The Cross Over Africa*. New York: Friendship Press, 1945.

Bosch, David. "The Question of the Mission of Today." *Journal of Theology for Southern Africa* (December 1972).

The Church's Mission in Rhodesia's Towns. 1958.

Cotton, Walter Aidan. *The Race Problem in South Africa*. London: Student Christian Movement Press, 1926.

Dadzi, Kuedu. "Africa: One Continent, Two Faces." *Black Business Digest* (July 1972).

Davidson, Basil. *A Guide to African History*. 2nd ed. New York: Doubleday and Company, Inc., 1971.

Dodge, Ralph E. *The Unpopular Missionary*. Westwood: Fleming H. Revell Company, 1964.

Drumbeats from Kampala. London: Lutherworth Press, 1963.

Flower, Ken. *Serving Secretly*. London: John Murray Publishers, Ltd., 1987.

Gann, L. H. *A History of Southern Rhodesia*. New York: Humanities Press, 1969.

"Harare Residents Criticise New Rents Exploitation." *Christian Mirror* (October 1970).

Hartzell, Joseph C. *The Africa Mission of the Episcopal Church*. February 1909.

"History of the United Methodist Church." *Umbowo* 55, no. 12 (December 1972).

James, Henry I. *Missions in Rhodesia Under the Methodist Episcopal Church*. Old Mutare: Rhodesia Mission Press, 1935.

Kobia, Samuel Mugika. *Origins of Squatting and Community Organizations*. Unpublished M.A. dissertation, 1978.

Machiwenyika, Jansen. *History and Customs of the Manyika People*. Unpublished manuscript. Trans. by W. S. Musewe, 1943.

"The Mission Extension of The United Methodist Church in Africa." *Umbowo* (October 1972).

"The Mission Extension of The United Methodist Church in Africa (1816–1896)." *Umbowo* (December 1972).

The Mission of the Church in Urban Africa. 1961.

Mitchell, J. Clyde. *An Outline of the Sociological Background to African Labour*. Ensign Publishers, Pvt. Ltd., 1961.

Moltmann, Jürgen. *Theology of Hope*. New York: Harper & Row, Publishers, 1967.

Mugabe, Robert. *Our War of Liberation*. Gweru: Mambo Press, 1983.

Murapa, Rukudzo. "Osagyefo Pan Africanist Leader." *Black World* (July 1972).

A New People, A New Church. Hertogenbosch, Holland: Dutch Missionary Council, 1980.

New World Outlook (November 1978).

Nyagumbo, Maurice. *With the People*. Salisbury: Mardon Printers [Pvt.] Ltd., 1980.

Parsons, R. T., and Parsons, Nwosu, *Christian Ministry—Vital Issues*. Ibadan: Abiodun Printing Works, 1965.

Pheko, S. E. M. *Christianity Through African Eyes*. Lusaka: Daystar Publications Ltd., 1969.

Ranger, T. O. *Revolt in Southern Rhodesia*. Evanston: Northwestern University Press, 1967.

———. *State and Church in Southern Rhodesia 1919–1939*. Salisbury: The Central Africa Historical Association, 1958.

———. *The African Voice in Southern Rhodesia*. Evanston: Northwestern University Press, 1970.

Rosenstock-Huessy, Eugen. *Out of Revolution: Autobiography of Western Man*. Norwich, CT: Argo Books, 1969.

Samkange, Stanlake. *African Saga*. Nashville: Abingdon Press, 1971

———. *Origins of Rhodesia*. New York: Frederick A. Prager, 1968.

"Scholars Debate Role of Corporations in Third World Economics." *The Christian Century* (29 November 1972).

Spady, James S. "The Ancient Zimbabwe Empire." *Negro History Bulletin* 34, no. 2 (February 1971).

Sundkler, Benght. *The Christian Ministry in Africa*. London: SCM Press Ltd., 1960.

————. *Bantu Prophets in Southern Africa*. London: Oxford University Press, 1961.

Taylor, William. *Story of My Life*. New York: Hunt and Eaton, 1896.

"What Christian Life Means." *The Missionary Review of the World* (May 1938).

Williams, Chancellor. *The Destruction of Black Civilization*. Dubuque: Kendall/Hunt Publishing Company, 1971.

Winter, Gibson. *The New Creation as Metropolis*. 2nd ed. New York: The Macmillan Company, 1966.

Index